Antique Radios

Restoration and Price Guide

David and Betty Johnson

Cover photograph:
Jim Lewis Photography
LaCrosse, Wisconsin

All other photography by the authors.

ISBN 0-87069-418-9
Library of Congress Catalog
Card Number 81-71053

10 9 8 7 6 5 4 3 2 1

Published by

Wallace-Homestead Book Company
1912 Grand Avenue
Des Moines, Iowa 50305

*To those radiomen of the 1920s who,
in spite of changing technology and fashion,
kept the old radios for us to enjoy in the 1980s.*

Acknowledgments

Thanks to everyone who helped in the writing and photographing of this book. Their cooperation was magnificent. Special thanks to DeLayne Rand, who processed, printed, and improved the photographs; Donna Glowcheski, librarian in Galesville, Wisconsin, who helped us locate information about early radios; Joe Pavek of the Museum of Wonderful Wireless in Minneapolis, who started us in the restoration of old radios and gave us many hours; Scott VanderHamm, Assistant Curator of the Museum of Science and Natural History in St. Louis; Robert Bodner of the Western Heritage Museum in Omaha; Glenn Hadsell and Cog Hogden, who willingly talked radio with us and answered many questions; Ervin Krogstad, who taught us how to fine-tune an Aeriola Sr.

Kennedy, model 220, 1922, TRF, commercial receiver. Photographed at St. Louis Museum of Science and Natural History.

Contents

Reprint of 1922 RCA catalog, Radio Enters the Home. *Courtesy of Vestal Press.*

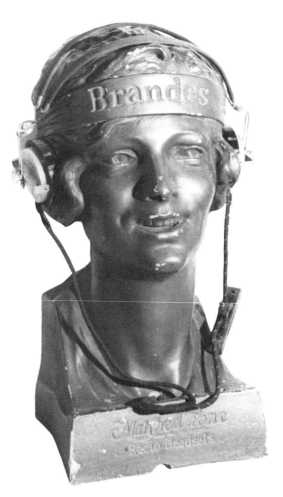

"Brandes Girl," earphone display head. Photographed at Western Heritage Museum.

Dictograph loudspeaker, 1922. Photographed at St. Louis Museum of Science and Natural History.

1 That Antique Radio—Is It Right for You?

There are many ways people begin to collect and restore old radios. Maybe they were given an old set or found one in an attic. Or they might have taken a fancy to one they saw at a garage sale or auction. No matter how an antique radio is found, its new owner will want to make it attractive and usable.

It's not difficult to improve the appearance of an old radio, and often it isn't hard to make it work well. But to do both, collectors will have to do some work and use their heads. This book contains tips and basic technical information about restoring old radio sets. You, the collector, will have to supply the work and the thinking. If you are confused by words in this chapter, use the Glossary near the end of this book or move on to the short course in electronics and radio in the next chapter.

Acquiring an antique radio is a personal thing. You must want the set you see. Ask yourself questions like these when you first see a prospect: "Would I enjoy having and using it?"; "Does it bring back memories of one I knew when I was younger?"; "Is it particularly handsome or unusual?"; "Do I think I can fix it?"

For information on what various sets are worth, in general and in particular, use the Price Guide near the end of this book. But remember, the most important question is "What is it worth to me?"

One warning is in order here. Watch out! Collecting and fixing radios can be habit forming, as the authors of this book so well know.

Determining Age

Appendix D includes detailed books on dating radios. We have space only for general information, here.

Primitive radios. The earliest sets were often homemade, using only one or two tubes, or no tubes at all. No attempt was made to make them pretty. They have historic value to the advanced collector but are not much fun for the beginner. Of course, if someone gives you one, don't throw it away!

Classical radios. Manufactured from about 1922 to 1928, classical radios were the first of the home entertainment receivers. Frequently they have many dials and are almost always battery powered. They use tube types like '01A, '12A, and '71A. They often have interesting cabinets. These radios can be fun but are quite rare and often expensive. Since they are battery powered and the correct batteries are no longer made, they will usually need to have power supplies built for them.

Mass market sets. These were made from about 1929

Grebe, model CR-8, 1922, battery, one tube, regenerative.

Freshman Masterpiece, 1925, battery, five tube, TRF. Photographed at St. Louis Museum of Science and Natural History.

Sleeper amplifier, type 3100, battery, two stage.

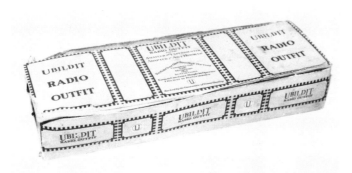

Early radio kit. Photographed at St. Louis Museum of Science and Natural History.

Typical A, B, and C batteries for radios from the late 1920s. Photographed at St. Louis Museum of Science and Natural History.

through 1946. During this period there was a nearly complete changeover to superheterodyne receivers and AC power sources. The only battery sets produced were portables and farm radios. Sets made during this era usually had wooden cabinets, many of which were very fancy. Their electronics were sometimes complex. These radios are fun to collect and use. They can often be bought for a reasonable price.

Postwar radios. These sets, made from about 1947 through 1960, aren't very interesting. Plastic cabinets prevail, and the wooden ones are only so-so. Radios of this era are inexpensive now and easy to fix. These aren't bad radios to get acquainted with as you develop your restoring skills.

Solid state sets. These radios, manufactured from about 1961 to the present, use transistors and integrated circuits rather than tubes. They are a whole new ballgame, and we will not discuss them in this book. They have no collectibility now, but may some day.

Your radio will need one of three types of power, depending partly on the set's age. The first of these is battery power. These are older portable radios, and they can be

identified by a bundle of wires emerging to join either a many-connection plug or metal lugs. While these are rather simple sets, they often require battery designs that are simply not available at any price. A power pack must be built for these sets in order to run them from the house AC line. For this reason, they aren't the best sets for beginners.

The second type, the AC set, is probably the one you will want to start with. When these are fixed, they are very usable. They can be identified by the line cord and plug, of course, and are usually quite heavy because they have a power transformer and chokes in the power supply. They have their own special problems for restorers but are still the best bet for beginners.

The third type is a special kind of AC set, the AC/DC receiver. This set has a line cord and plug but is usually much lighter in weight because it has no power transformer. Being cheaper sets, these frequently have plastic cabinets. They are very satisfactory to use. They can be easy to work on but are, under certain conditions, highly dangerous. Never test one outside its cabinet without reading the chapter on AC/DC sets in this book.

Determining Condition

You cannot thoroughly examine a radio until you get it home, but you can tell much before then about its condition by noting some problem signs that will affect both your decisions to buy and the price you'll pay.

Disasters

Cabinet in poor condition with large pieces of veneer or wood missing. There may be water damage to the veneer, and the wooden speaker grille may be broken with pieces missing. Small veneer problems can be solved, and some separation of veneer into layers can be glued. Likewise, broken grilles with pieces still there can be glued. You can do a lot with a cabinet, but not everything.

Radio chassis burned and blackened. Either the power supply has burned up or the set has been hit by lightning. The damage is usually too severe to repair.

Radio chassis badly rusted. Usually this, along with cabinet water damage, indicates that the set has been in water. Probably too many parts have been ruined to try fixing this set.

Possible Disasters

Extreme mouse damage. Many of the visible wires have been chewed, and it may look as if mice actually have been nesting in the radio. Some mouse damage can be fixed, but too much of it makes the set not worth the trouble.

Major parts missing. Some parts can be replaced but others, built for a particular set or model, may be hard to find. This is a judgment call. You must decide if you want to go to the effort of finding the parts. Many parts are, of course, replaceable without too much trouble.

Broken coils and castings. These hold parts in place and they can give real difficulty. Again, you need to use judgment. If you can imagine how to fix a part, you probably can do it.

Fixable

Missing tubes. Be sure you know what tubes are missing. Numbers and letters identifying the tubes may be stamped on the tube sockets or next to them. There may be a paper in the cabinet showing the tube layout. Most tubes can be replaced, although they may be expensive. The older types usually will cost more. If all the tubes are gone, you probably will be spending more than you want.

Rubber insulation flaking from wires. Wires can be replaced, so long as you know where they are going and where they came from.

Grille cloth missing or torn. Torn cloth may be mended if it is not too rotten. Replacement cloth can be installed easily.

Loudspeaker cone missing or torn. It may be possible to repair if the damage is not too great. Speakers can be professionally reconed, also.

Knobs missing. If one knob is there, it may be possible to match it or mold satisfactory replacements. You may be able to substitute different, but similar, knobs.

Atwater Kent, model 20, 1924, battery, TRF. Photographed at Museum of Wonderful Wireless.

RCA, Radiola III, 1924, battery, regenerative. Photographed at St. Louis Museum of Science and Natural History.

This list will help you make an educated guess about the radio you are considering. Of course, there may be invisible problems that only careful examination and testing will reveal, but you can tell much from a radio's appearance.

By the way, if you are buying at auction, don't put too much faith in what the auctioneer says. He may know very little about a set's condition.

RCA, Radiola IIIA, 1924, battery, regenerative. Photographed at St. Louis Museum of Science and Natural History.

David Grimes, Inverse Duplex 7, 1925, battery. Photographed at Museum of Wonderful Wireless.

Determining Price

When you have examined your prospective radio, try to make a guess of its overall condition. That, with the Price Guide in this book, will help you set the price you're willing to pay. Here are some condition guidelines.

Excellent. This radio is in perfect working condition. It may show a bit of wear. Knobs, dials, and case may show a little discoloring from age. This set is a rare find.

Very good. This radio is in working condition although it might not actually work when bought. There may be a few easily replaced parts, like a tube, a few screws, or a bad power cord. There may be some minor cabinet wear or marking. Its appearance is good, and if the price is right, it is a good buy.

Good. Most of the sets you find will be in this condition. They are either functioning or easily repairable. The cabinets may need refinishing. There will be some missing or broken parts, but they can be restored.

Fair. This radio does not work. It will need considerable effort, but it is repairable. It exhibits heavy wear and tear with many missing parts and, possibly, broken castings. Radios in this category present quite a challenge. They sell cheaply but are not for beginners. Don't pay too much for one of these.

Poor. This set will be close to impossible to repair since too many parts are missing, ruined, or damaged. The cabinet may show heavy damage as well. You've really got to want one of these to bother with it. Sometimes two sets of the same model in poor condition will provide enough parts to make one workable set, but generally speaking, these are junk.

Remember this grading guide when it comes to pricing and buying a set. Most prices in guides will be for sets that are in good to very good condition. Excellent sets may command a sizable premium, whereas poor radios can be had for very little and are, sad to say, often worth it.

DeForest, model F-5M, 1925, battery.

Kolster, model 6D, 1926, battery, TRF.

10

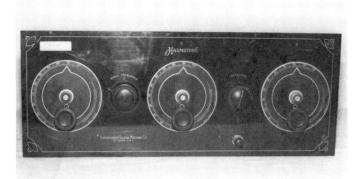

Harmotone, battery, St. Louis manufacturer. Photographed at St. Louis Museum of Science and Natural History.

Western Electric, carbon microphone, used in radio stations. Photographed at St. Louis Museum of Science and Natural History.

Atwater Kent, model 30, 1926, battery, TRF, open.

Northland, battery, Minneapolis manufacturer. Photographed at Museum of Wonderful Wireless.

Buy your set and take it home so you can examine and clean it. You probably will find a few more problems. After all, your new radio is between thirty and sixty years old, and that's quite old for electronic equipment. Don't expect everything to be perfect. We'll take repairing your radio a step at a time in the following pages.

Magnavox loudspeaker, model M-4, 1925.

Modern battery eliminator for battery sets, interior.

Grebe, model MU-1, 1925,
battery, five tube, TRF.

2 How Does a Radio Work?

In order to do even basic radio repair, it is helpful to know some electronics theory. This chapter will provide that. If you wish to learn more, stop at your local library or bookstore and look over their books on basic electronics.

Electron Theory

Briefly, all matter in the universe is made of about one hundred fundamental materials called elements. Some are common such as oxygen, hydrogen, carbon, and silicon. There are also rare and sometimes dangerous elements, such as radium. These elements in combination give us all familiar things. For example, oxygen and hydrogen combine to make water.

It is impossible to see single atoms because they are too small, but we know a good deal about how an atom is constructed. An atom has a central body of positive charge consisting of protons and neutrons. This nucleus is surrounded by an equal negative charge of much smaller electrons. The many different elements are the result of differing numbers of protons and electrons.

When electrons are pulled free of their atoms, an electric current is produced. In some substances, the electrons come loose quite easily, and these substances are called conductors. Since the charge of an electron is very small, many billions of them must be set in motion to produce a measurable current.

Electrons exist everywhere in nature, and loosely bound free electrons tend to be present in equal numbers in all places. But if a body has more electrons than do the bodies surrounding it, it is said to be negatively charged. On the other hand, if a body lacks enough electrons to be neutral, it is considered to have a positive charge.

If a positively charged body is brought into contact with a negatively charged body, there will be a flow of electrons from the negative to the positive until both bodies have the same number of free electrons and become neutral. Electrons are always attracted in the direction of a positive charge.

The charged bodies need not be brought into direct contact for the electrons to flow. A wire that acts as a conductor can connect them. Copper, because of its comparatively low price among good conductors, is used most frequently, but nearly all metals are fairly good conductors of electrons.

Resistance. Any conductor exerts a certain amount of opposition to the passage of electrons. This opposition is known as resistance. Silver, copper, and aluminum have little resistance. Iron has considerably more, and it may become hot when many electrons are retarded in their passage through it. A thick wire has less resistance than a thin wire of the same material because it has a greater cross section, that is, more area, for the electrons to move in.

Substances other than metals can have a very high resistance, permitting few electrons to pass through them. Most plastics, glass, rubber, and porcelain are good examples of common insulators.

The unit for measuring resistance is the ohm. Let us assume that we have a battery that is producing an electron pressure of one volt. It is connected to push a current through a wire with one ohm of resistance. The electron flow, or current, through the wire will be one ampere (amp). Voltage, resistance, and the resultant current are interrelated in any circuit. In circuits where the direction of electron flow does not change often (DC), the relationship is expressed mathematically according to Ohm's Law: $I = E/R$. The symbol I stands for the current in amps, E for the voltage in volts, and R for the resistance in ohms.

Sources of electron flow. Two practical ways of producing substantial electron pressure or voltage exist: chemical generation and magnetic generation. Chemical generation is possible because certain substances in reaction to other substances produce either a shortage or an excess of electrons between the different substances. The most common generators of this sort are batteries of the rechargeable, or single service, type. The current produced by this device always moves in one direction, and its pressure, or voltage, depends on the substances of which it is made.

Magnetic generation is the principle sort used commercially. A wire in a moving magnetic field will have an electron pressure produced between its ends and can thus provide a current flow. This is the principle behind all generators. Generators can be designed to produce almost any voltage of either one-way (direct) current or alternating current.

Electrical currents. These may flow in one direction only or they may change direction regularly. Single direction flow is called direct current (DC), whereas a current that changes at regular intervals is called alternating current (AC). The change from one direction to another in AC does

13

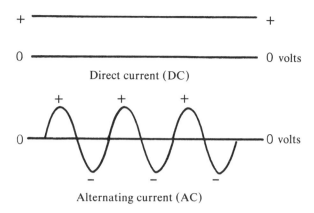

Direct current (DC)

Alternating current (AC)

1. Direct and alternating currents.

not happen instantaneously. Instead the flow will be wave-like, gradually increasing in intensity in one direction, then decreasing gradually to an absence of electron movement, followed by a reversal of current flow to a maximum and another decrease of current flow, and so on. The complete change from start to maximum and back is called one cycle, or hertz. Figure 1 will help you visualize this. The height of the curve shows voltage and rate of change through a complete positive and negative loop, or frequency. The frequency in U.S. power systems is generally 60 cycles per second at a voltage of about 115 v. Audio frequencies will vary from 20 cycles per second to 20,000 cycles per second. Radio frequencies will show rates of change of many thousands per second to many millions per second.

Magnetism. Another force that is important to radios and electrical devices is magnetism. Transformers, motors and generators, loudspeakers, and other radio parts make use of magnetism. Magnetism, like electricity, cannot be seen or felt, but its effects can be detected, measured, and used.

A magnet can attract iron or steel objects because it produces a force field. The magnet has two poles (ends) of opposite force, or polarity. If a magnet is brought close to a piece of iron, its force field produces an opposite field in the nearest end of the iron. The two oppositely magnetized poles attract.

In the same way, when two magnets are brought together, the oppositely magnetized poles will attract each other, whereas the similarly charged poles will repel each other. Figure 2 shows how this force field is visualized. The lines do not actually exist, but the force they show and its direction do.

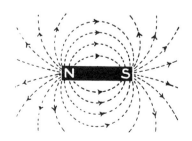

2. Magnetic field surrounding bar magnet.

An important property of the magnetic force field coming from a magnet's pole is that it decreases proportionately with the square of the distance from that pole. The strength of a field at 2″ from a pole will be one-fourth the strength at 1″. The field is strongest at the pole.

Magnetism can be produced by the flow of an electrical current through a conductor. This is just the opposite of what happens in a generator where the moving magnetic field produces an electric current. Every wire that carries a current has a magnetic field around it that is proportional to current strength and distance from the wire. By winding wire to form a coil, a much stronger magnetic field can be produced, since the field of each individual turn will add to the next and produce a stronger field, as you can see in figure 3. That coil has a field much like the magnet in figure 2.

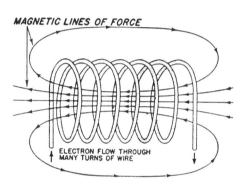

3. Coil with magnetic field.

As we saw before, the magnetic field, or flux, is thought of as imaginary lines of force from one end of the coil or magnet to the other. Total magnetic flux depends on the number of turns of wire and the strength of the current. If the current is high, fewer turns of thick wire will be required. If the current is weak, many turns of thin wire will be needed in order to produce the same magnetic force.

The magnetic flux of a coil can be increased greatly if a bar of iron is placed in the center of the coil, since the lines of force produced will be concentrated in the iron. A coil with an iron core will act exactly like a magnet, so long as current flows through the coil.

Inductance and reactance. The ability of a coil to set up a magnetic field when current is flowing through it is called inductance. A coil with current flowing will tend to oppose any increase or decrease of current flow. This opposition force in an inductance is called reactance and is proportional to the inductance of the coil. Inductance is measured in units called henries, and reactance is measured in ohms.

Reactance also depends on the rate of change of the current through the coil. A greater rate of change will result in greater opposition or reactance in a coil with a certain inductance.

A useful result of reactance is that it allows direct (unchanging) current to flow through it easily while resisting (or choking) changing or alternating, current.

If a coil with a magnetic field comes near another coil, an electrical pressure will be caused in the second coil, so long as the magnetic field is moving or changing. Energy will pass from one coil, called the primary coil, to the second, called the secondary coil, so long as the field in the first coil is changing in intensity. The ratio of the voltage in the two coils will be the ratio of the number of turns in those two coils. If the secondary coil has more turns than the primary, it will have a higher voltage than the primary. If it has fewer turns, it will have a lower voltage.

Thus, this two-coil device can be used to transform one voltage into another higher or lower one. For this reason it is called a "transformer," and it is one of the most useful devices in a radio set.

Capacitance. Two metal plates facing each other and separated by air or a thin insulation called a dielectric make a condenser, or capacitor. *Condenser* is the older term but *capacitor* more accurately describes the action of the device.

If such a capacitor is connected to a battery, electrons will flow from the plate connected to the positive terminal of the battery through the battery to the opposite plate. If the battery is disconnected, the electrons will be stored on one plate. If the plates are reconnected by wire, the electrons will flow through the connecting wire to the other plate, thus equalizing the charge of electrons on each.

The capacitance, or storage ability, of a condenser depends on three things: the size of the plates, the space between the plates, and the dielectric used. The larger the plate area, the greater the capacity. The closer the plates, the greater that capacity as well. Capacity also depends on the dielectric. For example, a capacitor of a certain physical size will have seven times the capacity with mica as an insulator as it would with air as the dielectric.

The unit of measurement of capacity is the farad. However, the farad is much too large a unit for radio work. A more useful unit is the microfarad (mfd.) which is 1/1,000,000 of a farad. An even smaller unit is also found, the micromicrofarad (mmfd.) which is 1/1,000,000 of a microfarad.

Capacitors or condensers not only store energy, but they are also important in radio for another reason. If a condenser is connected in a circuit with direct current being supplied, the condenser will permit current to flow for a very short time while it is being charged. If alternating current is supplied, the capacitor will permit current to flow to some degree because the charging voltage is constantly changing. The faster the change, the easier the flow. This opposition to slow change or direct current is called reactance and is measured in ohms. This reactance is called capacitive reactance, and it is different from the reactance of coils, which is called inductive reactance. In fact, these two kinds of reactance tend to cancel one another, a fact useful for tuning circuits.

Condensers used to block DC while passing a wanted AC signal are called blocking condensers. Condensers wired to pass AC to ground while keeping DC in the circuit are called bypass condensers. A variable capacity condenser used to tune a resonant circuit is called a variable condenser or tuning condenser.

Smaller capacitors used in old radios had waxed paper or mica as dielectric. Variable condensers generally make use of air or mica.

Another important type of condenser, the electrolytic, has a very high capacity for its size. This is because its dielectric is chemically formed when the condenser is subject to a charging voltage. This dielectric is very thin and is capable of withstanding high voltages. It is the thinness of the dielectric that gives the electrolytic its high capacity. These capacitors can be used as filters in power supplies and for low frequency bypass tasks.

Resonance. An especially useful result of the combination of inductance and capacity in a circuit is called resonance. The reactance of an inductance and the similar, but opposite, reactance of a condenser will both change with a change in the frequency of the alternating current flowing in them. At a certain frequency, called resonance, these two reactances will be equal and cancel one another. Depending on the way the capacity and inductance are wired together, that resonant frequency will either be strengthened while all others are reduced or it will be reduced more than all others. This principle can be used to tune a circuit to a desired frequency by varying either the capacity of the circuit or its inductance. Figure 4 shows how such a tuned circuit works.

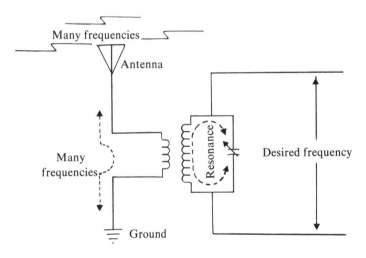

4. Frequency selection by tuned circuit.

Radio Tubes

The device that made radio transmission and reception truly practical was the vacuum tube. Ordinarily a receiving tube consists simply of two or more electrodes inside a high-vacuum glass or metal shell. The shell holds the vacuum necessary to maintain and control electron flow and keep filaments from burning.

You recall that electrons are invisible charges of negative electricity capable of traveling thousands of miles per second. These flowing electrons make radio tubes possible.

A tube contains a number of parts. The cathode is the element that supplies electrons. A directly heated cathode consists of a special wire coated with a substance that gives

15

off electrons when heated. The necessary heat is provided by passing an electric current through the filament wire. Examples of directly heated cathode, or filament, tubes are 45, 80, and '01A.

An indirect, or "heater," cathode tube has a heating element inside a metal sleeve from which it is electrically insulated. This sleeve is coated with a material that emits electrons. Most modern AC set tubes are of this kind. Typical tubes in older sets with this sort of cathode are 27 or 24A.

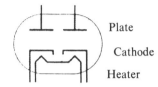

5. Dual section diode tube.

A diode tube has two working elements, a cathode to supply the electrons and a plate to attract and receive the flow. Shown in figure 5 is a tube with two diodes within the same shell. Since electrons are negative in charge, they are attracted by a positively charged plate and flow to it. If the plate, on the other hand, has a negative charge, no flow will take place. The diode acts as a one-way valve permitting electron flow in one direction only. Tube types 80, 6H6, and 35Z5 are examples of diodes. Diode tubes are used most frequently as rectifier tubes in power supplies or as detectors.

The triode is a three-element tube. The third element, called a control grid, is located between the cathode and plate and consists of a coiled wire with space between the loops (figure 6). The purpose of the grid is to control the

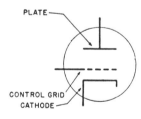

6. Triode tube.

flow of electrons to the plate. Since electrons are negative electrical charges, they are repelled and prevented from passing to the plate when a negative voltage is applied to the grid. When the grid becomes less negative it permits some electrons to pass to the plate. A change of even part of a volt on the grid is enough to either permit or stop the passage of electrons. The grid can easily vary the number of electrons moving through the tube. This ability of a small voltage change to effect a large current flow is called amplification. This important property makes it possible to increase very small signal voltages to usable levels. Any degree of amplification can be obtained simply by adding

more stages (tubes) in a series. A tube will also work over a wide range of frequencies and can amplify radio frequencies as well as audio frequency signals.

In actual operation the grid is usually kept slightly negative to limit the flow of electrons. When you tune in a station's program, you are actually picking up a small electrical charge and adding it to the grid voltage on your tube, making it more or less negative and decreasing or increasing the electron flow. But the signal you pick up is not constant. It varies with the speech or music fed into the broadcaster's microphone, so the varying flow of electrons between the cathode and the plate can duplicate the program. After detection and sufficient amplification, there is a signal strong enough to run a loudspeaker.

A triode tube is problematic, however. Some electrical capacity exists in the tube between the cathode and grid and the grid and plate. This acts as a small condenser wired between those parts and limits the possible amplification, or gain, of the tube. If too much amplification is demanded enough of the signal will be fed back through the capacity of the tube to make the tube start amplifying its own signal and begin oscillating at some unwanted frequency.

The invention of the tetrode tube solved this problem. The tetrode has four elements with two grids. The second grid, called a screen grid, is between the control grid and the plate (figure 7). It operates at a voltage similar to the plate,

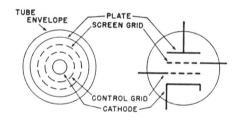

7. Tetrode or screen grid tube.

but receives no varying signal current. Thus it acts to shield the plate electronically from the grid. Instead of weakening the tube, this permits more amplification without oscillation.

Sometimes a third grid, called a supressor grid, is added between the screen grid and the plate. This makes a pentode tube (figure 8). A pentode is capable of even higher amplification than is a tetrode.

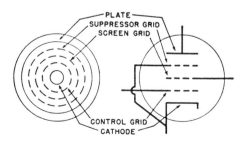

8. Pentode tube.

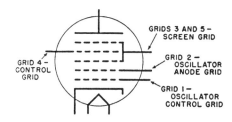

9. *Pentagid converter tube.*

as subtubes in the same electron stream. An example of this would be the multigrid converter tube shown in figure 9. Often a careful examination of the electrical circuit will help the repairer discover how a given tube works.

Circuit diagrams. Radio service information always includes a circuit diagram. This is a drawing showing the electrical paths within a radio, identifying wires with lines and parts with symbols. When you examine the diagrams in this book you will need to know the symbols. Figure 10 shows some of the common symbols used, particularly in older diagrams. Not all diagrams use identical symbols, but once you have used circuit diagrams a few times, you will be able to understand.

There are other tube types than triode and dual diode that will combine two or more working sets of elements in the same shell. Sometimes more grids are added and used

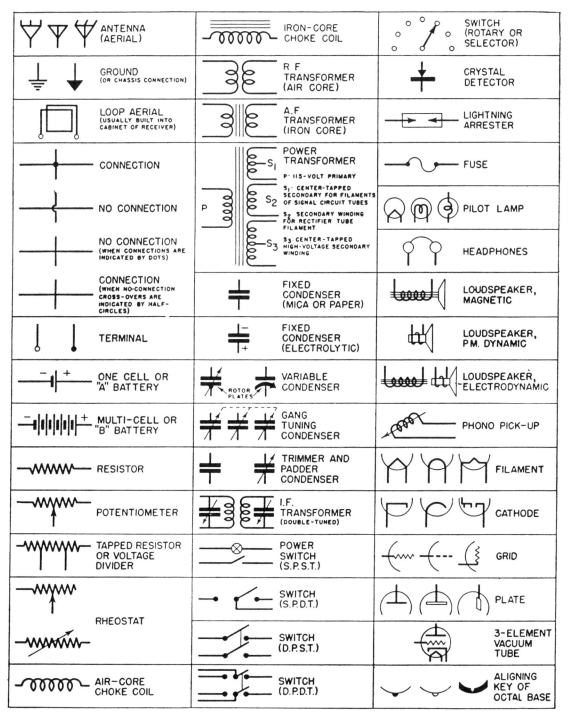

10. *Schematic symbols used in radio.*

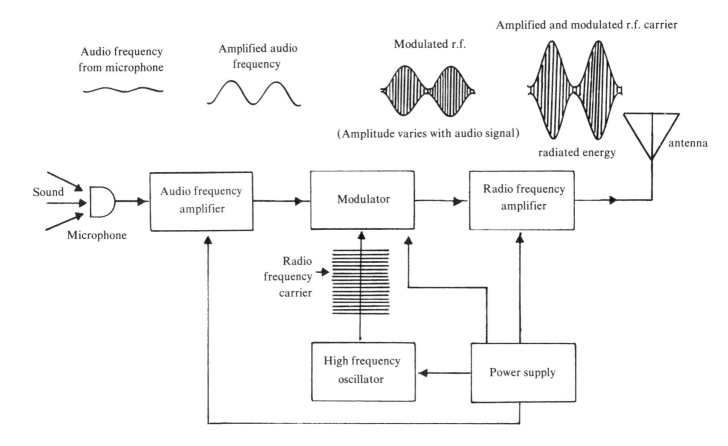

11. Basic transmitting station (block diagram).

Broadcasting and Receiving

In order to transmit a program, a radio broadcasting station must have several basic parts. Figure 11 is, of course, a simplified diagram. Much more is involved in a working station, but always there must be five basic parts.

● There must be some way to change sound pressure into an equivalent electrical signal. This is done by a microphone.

● There must be a section designed to generate a radio frequency (r.f.) alternating current of the desired carrier frequency. This is done by the oscillator section.

● There must be a section that will impress the audio frequency energy from the microphone onto the r.f. carrier. This is done by the modulator.

● There must be some device that will cause the modulated energy to be radiated into space. This is done by the transmitting antenna.

● There must be a source for the large amounts of energy required to transmit a strong signal. This is provided by the station's power supply.

A radio receiver must be provided with circuits that perform the opposite function of the transmitter. Figure 12 shows a basic receiver. Again, there are basic requirements.

● There must be some way of picking up the desired transmitted energy from space. This is done by the receiving antenna and the tunable circuits of the receiver.

● There must be some way of recovering the audio frequency (a.f.) signal from the modulated radio frequency (r.f.) carrier. This is the task of the detector.

● There must be some way of changing the audio frequency's electrical energy into sound. This is the function of the loudspeaker.

● There must, usually, be a source of electrical energy for the receiver. This is the function of the power supply.

You'll be working with receivers rather than transmitters, and probably with the superheterodyne. Figure 13 will give you an idea, in block form, of the parts that make a superhet. The signal moves through the circuit from top to bottom of the diagram.

The antenna, a loop or piece of wire, picks up a wide variety of radio signals. The strength of these signals is only

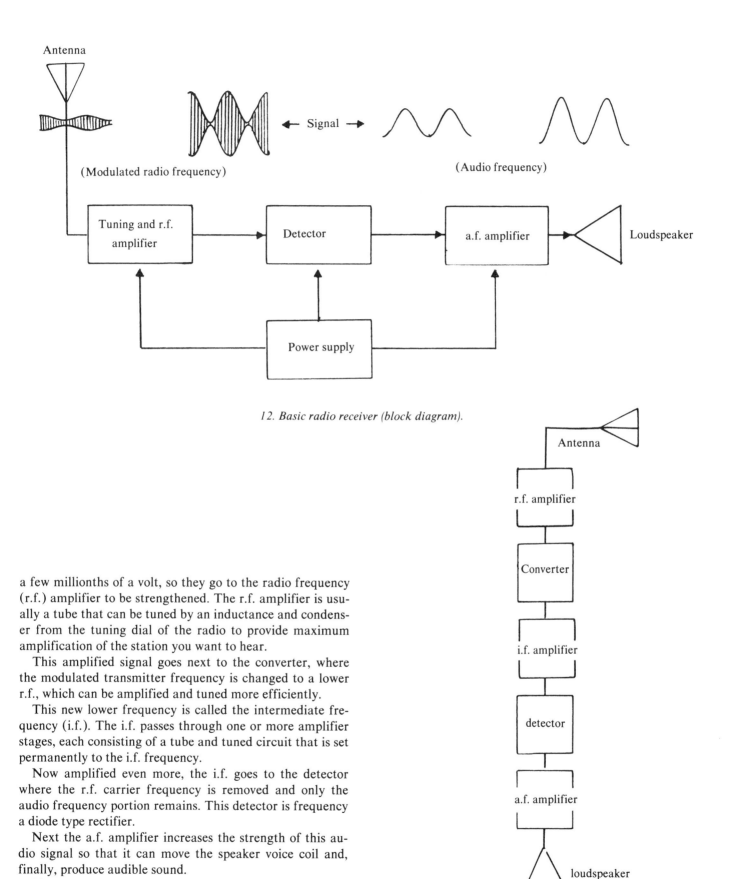

Antenna

(Modulated radio frequency)   ← Signal →   (Audio frequency)

Tuning and r.f. amplifier → Detector → a.f. amplifier → Loudspeaker

Power supply

12. Basic radio receiver (block diagram).

a few millionths of a volt, so they go to the radio frequency (r.f.) amplifier to be strengthened. The r.f. amplifier is usually a tube that can be tuned by an inductance and condenser from the tuning dial of the radio to provide maximum amplification of the station you want to hear.

This amplified signal goes next to the converter, where the modulated transmitter frequency is changed to a lower r.f., which can be amplified and tuned more efficiently.

This new lower frequency is called the intermediate frequency (i.f.). The i.f. passes through one or more amplifier stages, each consisting of a tube and tuned circuit that is set permanently to the i.f. frequency.

Now amplified even more, the i.f. goes to the detector where the r.f. carrier frequency is removed and only the audio frequency portion remains. This detector is frequency a diode type rectifier.

Next the a.f. amplifier increases the strength of this audio signal so that it can move the speaker voice coil and, finally, produce audible sound.

Simpler receiver designs were used in older sets. These are discussed, along with a more detailed explanation of the superheterodyne, in the chapter on receiver theory.

Antenna

r.f. amplifier

Converter

i.f. amplifier

detector

a.f. amplifier

loudspeaker

13. Superheterodyne receiver (block diagram).

Globe Duodyne radio advertisement, ca. 1927. Courtesy of Prairie Farmer.

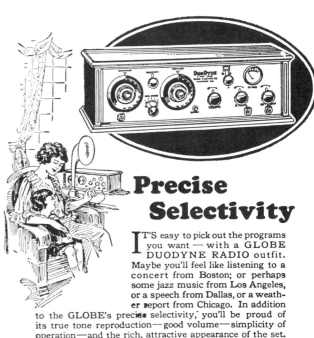

Precise Selectivity

IT'S easy to pick out the programs you want — with a GLOBE DUODYNE RADIO outfit. Maybe you'll feel like listening to a concert from Boston; or perhaps some jazz music from Los Angeles, or a speech from Dallas, or a weather report from Chicago. In addition to the GLOBE's precise selectivity, you'll be proud of its true tone reproduction — good volume — simplicity of operation — and the rich, attractive appearance of the set.

If there's no GLOBE dealer near you, write us for free illustrated literature which shows the various styles of GLOBE RADIO outfits. Price range to suit every purse.

GLOBE ELECTRIC CO., 18 Keefe Ave., Milwaukee, Wis.
Also Manufacturers of Globe Auto Batteries

GLOBE
DUODYNE RADIO

FADA
Radio

Play by play, vivid, clear, real!

It's new! It's startling! It's better!

Fada Harmonated Reception is as much better than ordinary radio as the electric light is better than the oil lamp!

For the first time every feature of both receiver and speaker have been thoroughly co-ordinated and protected.

Ask the Fada Dealer for a demonstration and hear *complete* reception for the first time. It's unbelievably good.

Fada Neutrodyne Receivers — table and furniture models — 8, 6 and 5 tube — ranging from $85 to $400. Fada Cone Speaker — Table type $35. Pedestal Floor type $50

Send for booklet "D" and name of the nearest Fada dealer

F. A. D. ANDREA, INC.
1581 Jerome Avenue, New York

Manufacturers of TUNED RADIO FREQUENCY Receivers using the highly efficient NEUTRODYNE principle

Fada Neutrolette. 5-tube tuned radio frequency receiver with neutrodyne improvements. Mahogany case. **$85**

Fada Neutrolette advertisement, ca. 1927. Courtesy of Prairie Farmer.

Ward's New Radio Catalogue Is Yours Free

This Catalogue represents the world's greatest radio store

Where you buy Radio is equally as important as the set you buy.

Send to Radio Headquarters for the most complete Catalogue of the season. See for yourself what is new in Radio and what has been actually tested and approved.

See for yourself what low prices can be made on Radio when it is sold without the usual "Radio profits."

A Complete Radio Manual

This new 52 page Radio Catalogue shows everything in parts, batteries, cabinets, contains a list of stations, a radio log for recording stations. It shows the best of the new sets. One tube sets that give amazing results. Five tube sets with a single dial to turn. Think of tuning in one station after another by turning a single dial!

Every price quoted means a big saving to you. Everything offered is tested by our own Radio Experts; in fact, the best experts compiled this Catalogue for you.

Write for this free 52 Page Book. It is yours Free.

Our 53 Year Old Policy

For 53 years we have sold only quality merchandise under a Golden Rule Policy. You can rely absolutely upon the quality of everything shown in this Radio Catalogue.

Write to the house nearest you for your free copy of Ward's new Radio Catalogue. Address Dept. 29-R

ESTABLISHED 1872

Montgomery Ward & Co.
The Oldest Mail Order House is Today the Most Progressive

Baltimore   Chicago   Kansas City   St. Paul   Portland, Ore.   Oakland, Calif.   Ft. Worth

Montgomery Ward Airline Radio catalog, 1925.

3 Cleaning It Inside and Out

The first thing to do with your new radio is to resist the temptation to plug it in. A good cleaning job now will make later work easier. Remember two rules: first, work in a well lit place and, second, be gentle. Clean your radio but don't scrub it. Don't move parts or wires any more than is necessary. You do not want to add to the problems your "new" radio might have.

You will need to remove the chassis, the metal base on which the radio itself is built. Unless the panel on which the controls are mounted is part of the chassis so that the whole thing slides out in one piece, remove the knobs. Many knobs have a small screw on the side. Use a small screwdriver to loosen the screw and remove it. Unless all the knobs are identical, make a diagram and number them so you can replace them in their former positions. If a knob has no screw, it is designed to pull off. Be careful because it may stick. If you pry off a knob with a screwdriver, protect the panel and do not break the knob. Plastic knobs may be brittle.

The chassis may simply lift from its cabinet. More often it will be screwed into the bottom. If you turn over the set to loosen these screws be careful to support the chassis and protect it from a fall. Before actually removing the chassis, check to see where the loudspeaker is attached. If it is connected directly to the chassis, leave it and remove the complete unit. If the loudspeaker is fastened to the front of the cabinet, unplug the cords that attach it.

Any wires remaining attached to the cabinet may be antenna wires. Unfasten them from the chassis, labeling the place of their attachment. If the wires lead to switches on the cabinet, the switches must be removed with the chassis.

Once it is free, clean the chassis, beginning on top and using a vacuum cleaner and soft paintbrush. Carefully and gently dust all reachable crevices and cracks with the paintbrush, using the vacuum to remove debris. Remove one tube at a time to avoid confusion and dust its socket. Remove and replace each tube several times to clean socket contacts. Clean tubes with a damp cloth, taking care not to rub off identification numbers.

Turn over the chassis. If the bottom is clean, leave it alone. Even if it is dirty, do not vacuum it directly. Use the soft brush again to remove accessible dirt. You may vacuum up debris, but keep the cleaner away from parts and

Atwater Kent speaker, type 2, 1926.

Atwater Kent, model 30, 1926, battery, six tube, TRF.

wires. Insulation on wires may be very brittle and could flake off.

Clean the cabinet with thorough use of the vacuum brush. Use the crevice tool and paintbrush to get into corners. Dust thoroughly to remove as much loose matter as possible. Then clean it—inside and out, top and bottom—with a cloth dampened in turpentine. Dry all surfaces. If veneer is coming loose, use care. Be careful around the cloth covering the speaker opening, also. A light dusting will suffice.

Before you set the cabinet aside, remove the loudspeaker. It will be needed for later testing with the chassis. Again, the speaker may simply lift from the cabinet or it may be bolted or screwed to the cabinet panel. Clean the speaker as carefully as you did the chassis. *Caution*: The paper cone on the speaker will probably be brittle and easily damaged.

Now store the clean cabinet until the radio is repaired and working. Your next step is a careful examination of the chassis.

Crosley, model RFL 60, 1926, battery, five tube, TRF.

RCA Radiola 18, 1927, AC, TRF. Photographed at St. Louis Museum of Science and Natural History.

Atwater Kent, model 35, 1926, battery, TRF, top view.

Atwater Kent, model 35, 1926, battery, TRF, front view.

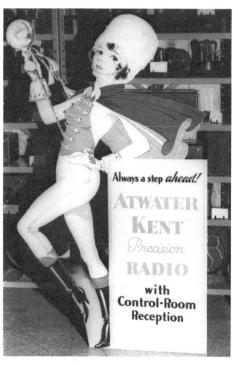

Atwater Kent display. Photographed at Museum of Wonderful Wireless.

RCA, Radiola 100A speaker, 1926. Photographed at St. Louis Museum of Science and Natural History.

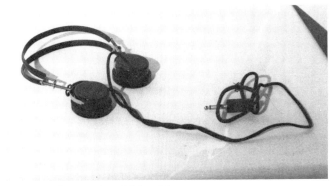

Trimm professional model headphones.

Metrodyne, Super 7, 1926-27, seven tube, battery, TRF. Photographed at Museum of Wonderful Wireless.

Control panel, Atwater Kent, model 33.

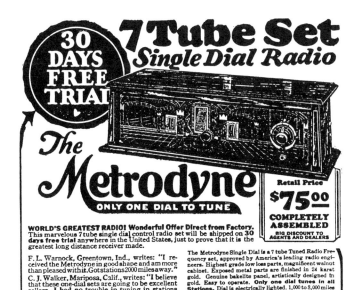

Metrodyne Super 7 advertisement, 1926.

Atwater Kent, model 33, 1927, battery, TRF, open. Clifford Fossum, owner.

23

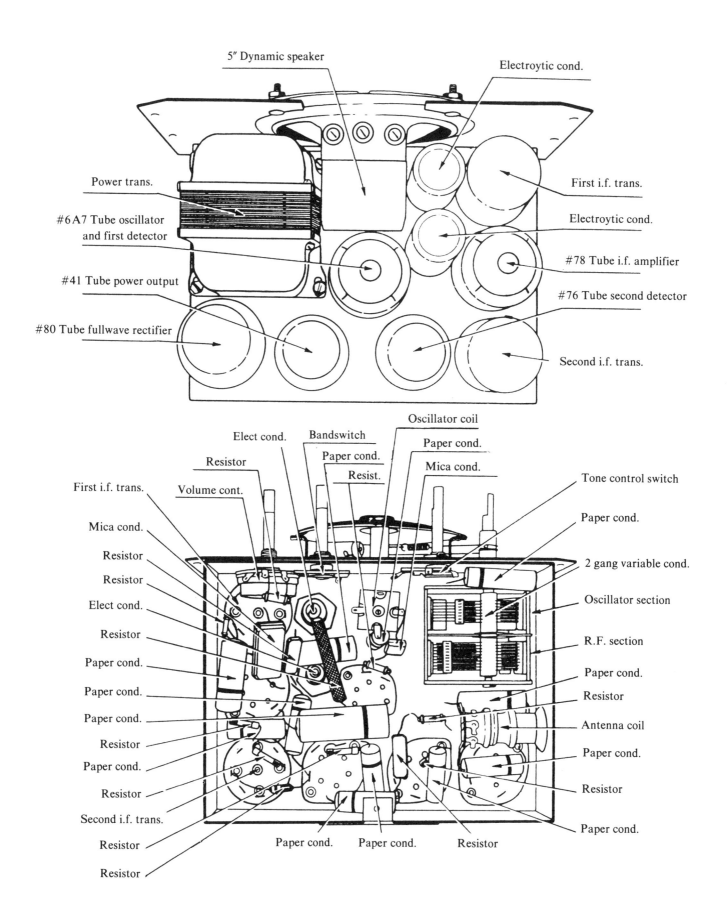

5″ Dynamic speaker

Electroytic cond.

Power trans.

First i.f. trans.

#6 A7 Tube oscillator and first detector

Electroytic cond.

#41 Tube power output

#78 Tube i.f. amplifier

#80 Tube fullwave rectifier

#76 Tube second detector

Second i.f. trans.

Oscillator coil

Elect cond.

Bandswitch

Paper cond.

Resistor

Paper cond.

Mica cond.

Resist.

First i.f. trans.

Volume cont.

Tone control switch

Mica cond.

Paper cond.

Resistor

2 gang variable cond.

Resistor

Oscillator section

Elect cond.

R.F. section

Resistor

Paper cond.

Paper cond.

Resistor

Paper cond.

Antenna coil

Paper cond.

Paper cond.

Resistor

Paper cond.

Resistor

Second i.f. trans.

Resistor

Paper cond.   Paper cond.   Resistor

Paper cond.

Resistor

14. Superheterodyne receiver typical chassis (top and bottom views).

4 Examining It

As you cleaned your radio, you probably took the first steps in examining it. But a thorough examination is important—it can save you from later grief. Many of your set's problems or faults will be visible if you look at it carefully in a good light. As you examine your set, remember that there is an orderly flow of electrical energy through it. There is nothing mysterious about it. Take the time to write down everything. If you remove a wire, make a note of where it came from. Use bits of colored tape to code wires and their connections. Keep notes and draw pictures of anything you change. Don't trust your memory! If you find yourself getting frustrated or tired, quit for a time. That radio has been waiting many years for you to come along; it can wait a few more days.

Figure 14 shows top and bottom views of a typical "midget" superheterodyne radio manufactured in the mid-1930s. As you examine the parts of your set, compare them with the drawings and try to identify each part of your set.

If anything seems to be wrong with a part, see the chapter on repair in this book. Here are some readily visible things that can tip you off to trouble.

Tubes. Order missing tubes immediately. You can't do anything without them. If you have access to a tube tester, check the tubes that remain, but remember that a tube may test all right and still not work in a particular radio.

Tuning condensers. Figure 15 illustrates a variable condenser and small mica trimmer condensers. Try to turn the tuning knob on your set. If it does not move, don't force it. Use TV tuner-cleaner spray on the points where shafts should move. Follow with a little WD-40 once the system is freed. Check for bent plates on the condenser and straighten them carefully if they are binding.

If the dial cord is broken, discover how it connected the tuning shaft and consenser. If you can't, you will have to obtain service instructions for your set. If it needs replacing use proper dial cord, if possible. (Sometimes heavy nylon thread will substitute.) If the dial cord slips where it loops around the tuning shaft, rub the cord at that point with a small amount of powdered rosin. When work on the tuning condenser is completed, turn the movable plates so that they are inside the fixed plates to prevent accidental damage. By the way, if you have to wait to get dial cord or a service diagram, you can still test the set by turning the condenser by hand.

Electrolytic condensers. Figure 16 shows some typical styles, but electrolytic condensers come in all shapes and sizes. They filter the direct current used by the tubes in

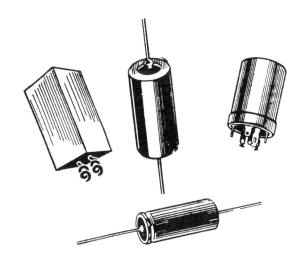

16. Electrolytic condensers.

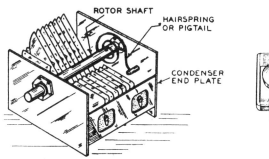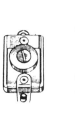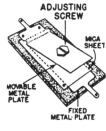

15. Variable and trimmer condensers.

your set. They are usually marked with rather high capacities, in the range of 4 to 50 microfarads (mfd.), as opposed to similar-looking paper condensers, which are usually .5 microfarad capacity or less. Corroded or swollen electrolytic consensers are worthless. Replace them with units of equal or greater capacity and equal or greater working voltage. Newer filter condensers are much smaller than the original parts. It's a good idea to replace suspicious-looking elements before you try out your set.

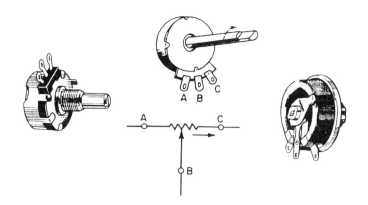

18. Volume controls and rheostats.

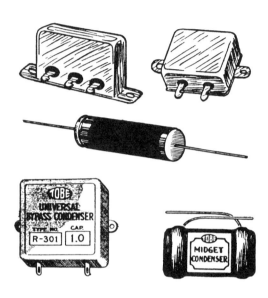

17. Paper condensers.

Paper condensers. Figure 17 shows some typical styles. They may be in square metal cans or in plastic tubes or rectangles, but most often are in cardboard tubes sealed with wax. It is hard to tell if they are bad by looking. If a wax-filled one has lost all wax out of the ends, it has probably shorted and should be replaced. Paper condensers used in bypass situations where a high voltage is on one side are prone to failure. The capacity and working voltage will usually be printed on the condenser. Replace with plus or minus 25 percent the same capacity and the same or greater working voltage. Modern condensers, or capacitors, are much smaller and better. Often they are small enough to be put inside the case of the old part, if you want to be strictly authentic.

Mica condensers. These small plastic rectangles are very reliable because of their good dielectric. They may sometimes open but seldom short-circuit.

Volume controls and rheostats. Figure 18 shows examples. These variable resistors have their own problems. Wire-wound units break and carbon controls become dirty and noisy. This is noticeable as a scratching sound when the radio is on and the control is turned. To rectify this, spray a good TV tuner-cleaner into the control. In fact, spraying all controls in this manner is a good idea. Faulty volume controls aren't detectable by eye. Tone controls behave in the same way and have the same problems.

Resistors. Figures 19, 20, and 21 give examples of two basic types of resistors and the color code used to mark resistance of carbon resistors. Wire-wound resistors usually carry quite a bit of power. Problems with them are often caused by a broken wire in the resistance element. Units with the resistance wires in the open are likely to corrode,

19. Carbon resistors.

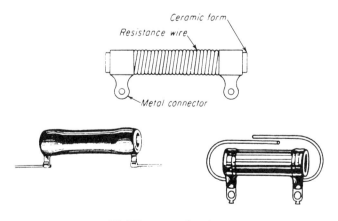

20. Wire-wound resistors.

26

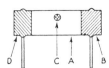
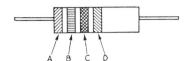

Color	Figure
Black	0
Brown	1
Red	2
Orange	3
Yellow	4
Green	5
Blue	6
Violet	7
Gray	8
White	9

Color A	Gives first figure of resistor value.
Color B	Gives second figure of resistor value.
Color C	Gives number of ciphers following the first two figures.
Color D	Gold band indicates plus or minus 5 percent tolerance.
	Silver band indicates plus or minus 10 percent tolerance
	No band indicates standard plus or minus 20 percent tolerance.

21. Carbon resistor color code chart.

but units sealed in ceramic are reliable. Carbon resistors are smaller and are nearly always color-coded. About the only fault you will see in one is burning, which requires replacement. Also, there will probably be a fault in the tube or condenser that drew too much current through the resistor and caused the burning. Unfortunately, when a resistor burns, so does its color code, and a circuit diagram is necessary to regain that information. With experience, however, you can often make an educated guess.

Transformers and chokes. Figures 22, 23, and 24 show examples. These are easy to identify since they have iron cores and are bulky. They may be used to provide correct voltages for the set or to connect stages. Unless they have burned badly and are charred, it is difficult to tell by looking at them if they are all right. They may leak a little wax or tar with age, but this does not always indicate trouble.

23. Typical audio transformers.

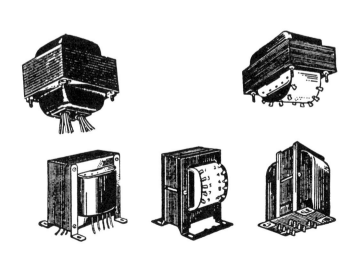

22. Typical power transformers.

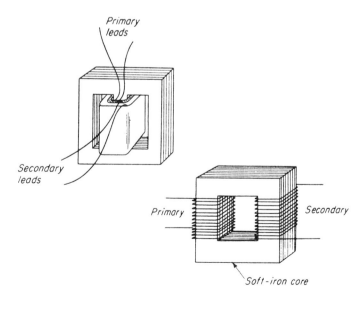

24. Iron core transformer construction.

27

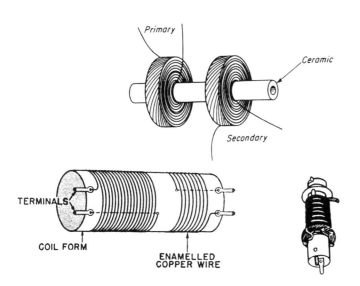

25. Radio frequency transformers and coils.

Radio frequency transformers and coils. Figure 25 shows examples. These come in all shapes and sizes. Some are shielded inside aluminum cans. Some are open and, usually, covered with a thick coat of wax. Most frequently, they couple antennas to the radio and interconnect radio frequency stages. If they are burned, they must be replaced. Beyond that, it is difficult to see faults. Note: If there are any screw adjustments with the coil or transformer, do NOT adjust. Some of these adjustments are critical, and since they were originally correct, probably they are still close. Wait until the set is running before touching these.

Loudspeakers. Examples are shown in figure 26. Sets made in the 1920s had many strange ways of converting the audio tube's electrical signal into sound, but by the 1930s, the dynamic speaker was almost universal. Two types of dynamic speakers are common. One type produces the necessary strong magnetic field for the voice coil to act on by means of a large coil of wire, called the field coil. This obtains power from the radio's high voltage power supply. Sometimes it acted as a filter choke in that supply. In some sets the field coil had its own power supply. Later, strong permanent magnets were developed, and these replaced the field coil as a source for the magnetizing field.

Small rips in the brittle cone can be repaired now with household glue or magic mending tape, after you have dusted carefully the surface to be fixed. Check to see if the cone is warped by placing your hands at nine and three o'clock while facing the front of the speaker. Place your thumbs near the center of the speaker and gently push in the cone. It should spring out again without any rubbing noise if it is not warped. If warped, see the chapter on repair in this book. Electrical faults in the speaker will be invisible.

Switches. These will be either enclosed power switches or open contact tone, band, or phono switches. Sometimes a sticking power switch can be freed if you spray some TV tuner-cleaner into it and switch it off and on several times with the power unplugged. Open switches are often corroded. Spray contacts with TV tuner-cleaner and operate the switch. Cut narrow strips of bond paper, push them between closed contacts, and slide the paper in and out to polish the contacts.

Wire. Check the power line and plug. If it is rubber and rotted, replace it now with similar style of wire. If the plug is removable, attach it to the new wire. Examine chassis wires. If they are cloth-insulated, they will give you no problems. If they have rubber covering, it will have hardened. If some insulation has flaked off and the wire is touching any metal, the wire will have to be either replaced or taped. Once you start to do that, the hardened insulation will fall off rapidly. So long as insulation is in place, even if it is hard, it will do its job.

Use your judgment throughout your examination of the radio. Do not replace anything that is not obviously bad. Remember to write down anything you think might cause problems later. And remember that great motto of the radio service profession: "If it ain't broke, don't fix it."

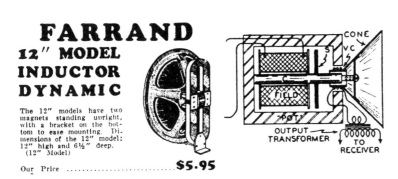
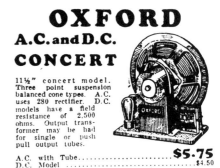
26. Loudspeaker construction and examples.

5 Trying Out Your Radio

If you have given your radio a careful examination and repaired obvious problems like bad power cords or disconnected wires, then you are ready to try out your set.

Remember the basic rules you learned in the last chapter; use your eyes, use your head, write everything down, and don't work too long. These apply to the things you will be doing from now on as well.

The first time you turn on a radio is always a bit frightening. Now you will find out what you really have. It is good to remember that there was probably one thing that went wrong with the set, putting it out of action and into the attic. During the years your radio has been in storage, other parts may have deteriorated also. Don't expect perfect results the first time you try. Your goal will be to find that one thing that stopped your set in the first place. What you want now is to get a station to come through the set, however faintly. After that you can tune it up and work at improving reception.

The easiest sets to test, once you have correct voltages, are the battery sets. Make sure the set is turned off and that all rheostats are turned fully counterclockwise. Hook up the power, making sure that you have the right polarity. That means that positive (+) sides of batteries or power supplies go to + terminals and negative (-) sides to - terminals. See to it that you have the correct voltages as well. If your voltages are correct, you probably will not hurt anything when you power up. You can turn on your set, turn up the rheostats about halfway, and go to the "What to Listen to and Look for" section in this chapter.

When you fire up an AC set you must be careful or you may literally fire it up. Applying full line voltage immediately could cause damage to the set's power supply. It's far better to bring an AC set's power supply to full voltage slowly, using a variable voltage isolation transformer. These units are costly (See Appendix A), but they allow you to increase the line voltage on a radio a few volts at a time. The isolation transformer also has its own fuse in case the radio has none. The voltage on the set is increased slowly until the set barely begins to operate or some fault becomes apparent.

Another way to protect an old power supply is to make a series light tester. This allows you to place a high-wattage light bulb or a fuse in series with the line to the radio. (See Appendix A for the design of such a tester.) The power supply may not operate with the series bulb or the voltage

may be too low for the rectifier tube to conduct, but you will get some indication of your radio's condition. If the bulb lights to full brightness when you turn the radio on, you have a problem in the primary circuit of the power supply. If the light does not go on at all, you have an open circuit in the primary circuit.

If it lights somewhat dimly, let the set operate that way for a time. You may see a dull glow in the tubes and you may have enough B voltage for the set to give some indication that it is alive. After you have run this way for ten or fifteen minutes with no problems or odors, you can apply full power. You might replace the bulb with a 5 amp screw-in fuse if you can get one.

Caution: High voltage. The power supply of an AC set is designed to handle power at high voltages. This can kill. These voltages make it necessary for you to be very careful when working in the power supply. If you suspect any problem, use a multitester to check voltages. Touch nothing without knowing its voltage. Never touch anything with one hand while touching the chassis with the other. If you do not own a multitester, get one. (See Appendix A for suggestions.)

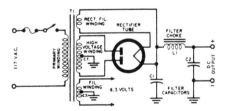

27. Typical power supply circuit diagram.

Figure 27 shows the circuit diagram of a typical AC power supply. Through the years, the insulation in the power transformer of your set may have broken down. Corrosion may have caused voltage divider resistors to open. The filter condensers will almost certainly have dried and work poorly. Sometimes these filters will regain some of their original filtering capacity after a few minutes of use, but they usually need replacement.

Remember, any unwanted connection between the high voltage (+) side and the ground of the set will cause the power supply to overheat. The problem may be in the power supply itself, due to an internal short circuit in a filter choke or, more likely, a bad filter condenser between B+ and ground. The problem may also be caused by a faulty bypass condenser or another part in the receiver.

An excessively high current drawn from the high voltage power supply will result in overheating of the transformers or resistors in the supply and in the rectifier tube plates becoming red-hot. The filament of the rectifier should, of course, glow red. If you see flashing purple or a purple glow in the rectifier tube, your rectifier tube is failing. Turn off your set until you know what is wrong. The chapter on troubleshooting will give you some tips on isolating the problem. Suspect the filter condensers first if you have any problem and replace or test them.

Much the same things will apply to an AC/DC set power supply. Before working with an AC/DC radio outside its cabinet, see the pertinent section in the next chapter. AC/DC sets can be particularly dangerous.

What to Listen to and Look for

Let's assume that you have powered up your set and nothing bad is happening in the power supply. Now is the time to use your ears. Put an antenna wire and a ground on your set, if it is not equipped with a loop antenna and has connections for outside ground and antenna.

Remember that every receiver has three basic sections besides its power source. One is the radio frequency section, which amplifies and selects the wanted radio frequency received from the antenna. Next is the detector, which recovers the audio signal from the radio frequency transmission. Finally, there is the audio frequency section, which amplifies the audio frequency electrical signal and changes it into audible sound.

After your radio has been on for at least five minutes, turn up the volume control gradually to full (clockwise) and listen to the loudspeaker. if you hear no hiss or soft hum, you have something wrong in either the speaker, the audio, or the power sections of your radio. The next chapter will help you troubleshoot those sections.

If you hear a soft hiss or hum but not stations, even as you tune over the dial, you have trouble in the r.f. or detector sections. The problem may also be caused by low power supply voltages in those sections. Your audio section is probably all right.

If you hear soft static or a weak station, you may have a problem in any section, but the overall condition of the set is not too bad. Check out the audio section by touching the grid of the first audio tube, usually the second tube back from the loudspeaker, with a screwdriver or your finger. If the volume control is turned up and the power and audio sections are okay, you will hear a fairly loud buzz.

Once you guess the troublesome section in your radio, check voltages and use the troubleshooting tips in the next chapter to find and fix the problem.

One more obvious problem may emerge. Your set may be making a squealing or loud putt-putt sound. If your set has a regenerative detector, the squeal shows that it is working but is not tuned correctly. More likely such a squeal results from the loss of some shielding. A putt-putt sound, called motorboating, results from a bad filter or bypass condenser or a broken connection to or in a volume control.

Once you realize what your problems are by reading this chapter and the next, you can evaluate the nature of the repairs you need to make. There are several ways to fix a set, depending on its age, value, and the seriousness of its problems. We want to restore the radio. But what exactly does that mean? A look at different levels of restoration will help you decide which is most practical for you.

Levels of Restoration

Replacement. This involves putting a modern radio and speaker in an old cabinet. It might be a good way to rescue an old cabinet, but it destroys any value your set may have as an antique radio. Don't do it unless there is nothing that can be done to save the old radio and the cabinet is exceptionally fine. (Of course, if you find an empty cabinet you like. . . .)

Modification. This means that you make changes in the actual design of the circuit to incorporate modern concepts. You might modify the circuit to use modern tubes. You might remove an old vibrator power supply and replace it with a modern solid state supply. Most of these modifications are highly technical and would not be tackled by most restorers. It is best not to modify an old set. It is all right, however, to use a modern external battery eliminator to run an old battery set because this involves no modification to the actual radio set.

Functional repair. This means that you replace faulty components with modern counterparts that perform the

RCA, Radiola 103 speaker, 1927. Photographed at St. Louis Museum of Science and Natural History.

same function in the circuit and make no attempt to hide the fact that you have done so. These are probably the easiest sorts of restorations to make. Sometimes when this is done, the old part will be left in place unwired, for appearance's sake. There is a fair chance that the set you restore may already have had such repairs in the past. Functional repair will lower the value of your set somewhat, especially if it is one from the classic era.

Practical restoration. This means that you make every attempt to produce a repair that looks original. New components may be lurking in old cases, but they will look original. Wire, knobs, and other visible parts will be authentic-looking even if they are reproductions. Tubes will not only be of the correct type, but will date from the correct era as well. This is the most practical restoration method, and sometimes, it is the only possible one. In the interest of the history of the set, keep a complete written record of all your work. You may wish to undertake a total restoration in the future. If the cabinet is refinished in a practical restoration, original type finishes must be used.

Total restoration. This means that only original parts or, if originals are not available, identical modern reproductions may be used. It may take years and several junked radios of the same type to do a total restoration. It can be a lifetime project.

Most restorers will make functional repairs or do a practical restoration, depending on the worth of the set. But whatever you do, keep careful records of your work. We keep parts we've removed along with restored sets in our collection. At some future date, you might upgrade a set from a functional repair to a practical restoration. Then the original parts will be useful.

Magnetic loudspeaker, date and make unknown.

Tower speaker ("Adventurer"), 1927. Photographed at Museum of Wonderful Wireless.

RCA, Radiola 60, 1928, AC superheterodyne. Photographed at Museum of Wonderful Wireless.

Crosley, model 608, ("Gembox"), 1928, AC, TRF.

Temple loudspeaker, model 15, 1929. Photographed at Museum of Wonderful Wireless.

Sparton, model AC-7, AC, closed. Photographed at Western Heritage Museum.

Sparton, model AC-7, AC, open.

6 Troubleshooting and Repairing

If you have reached this chapter, you probably have run into some problems. If you can obtain a circuit diagram for your radio, it will be a help. If you do not have a multitester (volt-ohm-milliampmeter) you probably want to get one. It may help you to know the probability of failure of various parts. Service literature estimates that at least two-thirds of all receiver troubles in modern tube type radios result from tube failure, so this is the first area to check. Of the remaining third of receiver troubles, bypass, filter, tone, and other condensers operating at high voltage account for 12 percent; transformers of all types account for 8 percent; resistors, particularly those operating at high temperatures, for 5 percent; switches for 5 percent; loudspeakers for 2 percent; and miscellaneous for 1 percent. In radios that have been stored a long time, the failure of condensers and any parts subject to corrosion, such as wire-wound resistors and switches, is likely to increase.

Basic Troubleshooting

In troubleshooting a radio, the first thing to do is check the basic voltages. Even without a circuit diagram you can guess what these should be. You have filament or heater voltage if the tubes light. On r.f. amplifier tubes, the plate (B) voltage will be somewhere between 45 and 200 volts, with battery sets having the lower voltages. A triode detector will usually have a low B voltage. On battery sets it may be as low as 22 volts. Audio stages will require B voltages of 67 to 250 volts with battery sets having, again, the lower voltage. A circuit diagram will give you more specific information.

If voltages seem close to normal, the next step in troubleshooting requires some source of signal. In audio stages an audible signal is needed. Often a screwdriver or finger touching the control grid will provide enough hum for a test. For r.f. and detector stages, a suitable r.f. signal is needed. Sometimes touching a grid with a bit of metal will cause an audible click. It is better to use some regular source of signal, however. (See Appendix A for signal generators and signal injectors.) Your process is to start with the last audio stage, prove that it works, and then move stage by stage back toward the antenna. Lacking a tube tester to check the tubes, you may still be able to find a faulty tube in this way.

One particularly annoying problem is the intermittent fault when the radio works only part of the time. When you are tracking an intermittent fault, take note of what happens when the set goes bad. Try to guess which section is causing the trouble. Almost any part can be the cause.

Some intermittents are heat sensitive and appear when the set is warm. Warm your set thoroughly and trace the problem when it occurs. Often intermittents are vibration sensitive as well. Try tapping or wiggling leads. (Swearing at the set may also produce some action.) Another common cause of intermittent operation is corroded solder joints. These can often be found by examining and wiggling wires. Once found, the joint can be resoldered. Bad switch contacts can act up intermittently. This is a common problem in old sets. Working the switch or wiggling its shaft will often show the fault. Even tubes may give trouble when they are warm. Tapping them will often show the fault.

An important aid in finding and fixing problems is an analysis of the different kinds of problems that accompany different types of receivers. The causes for the problems under each of the following sections are listed in approximate order of frequency, with the first item under each problem the most likely cause, and so on. Not every solution will apply to every set, of course, since a particular radio may not have the part mentioned.

Common Radio Problems

Problem: Receiver completely dead.
- Defective tube or tubes.
- Defective power supply. (See following sections on receiver type.)
- Bad "tone" condenser between plate of output tube and ground.
- Open cathode resistor in power amplifier tube circuit.
- Bad output transformer.
- Bad voice coil in loudspeaker.

Problem: Receiver makes some sound, but no program is received.
- Weak or bad tube, probably in r.f. or detector section.
- Defective filter or bypass condensers reducing B voltage.
- Defective audio frequency coupling condenser.
- Oscillator or converter in superhet receiver not functioning properly. Try a new tube.

- Short-circuited tuning condenser. Look for dirt or bent plates.
- Tuned circuits out of alignment.
- R.f, i.f., or a.f. transformer open or shorted to ground.
- Open plate load resistance in audio tube.
- Antenna terminal or coil short-circuited to ground.

Problem: Received stations are weak.

- May be caused by any of the difficulties listed under preceding problem.
- Inefficient antenna system.
- Open antenna coil. Try feeding antenna directly to grid of first r.f. tube or mixer.
- Weak magnet in permanent magnet (p.m.) speaker or field coil in electrodynamic speaker.

Problem: Excessive hum.

- Difficulty in power supply. (See receiver type below.)
- Open control grid circuit in audio stage.
- Cathode to heater short in a tube.
- Bad tube. This will often be a gassy rectifier or output tube. You can spot these by a distinct purple glow in the tube.

Problem: Motorboating (putt-putt sound), or oscillation (squeal), or distorted sound.

- Bad bypass or audio frequency coupling condenser.
- Open volume control resistance element.
- Tube shield(s) missing or not making good contact with base.

Problems of Battery Receivers

Problem: Radio completely dead. Tubes do not light even with volume control turned up.

- Batteries dead. Check voltages with set turned on.
- Bad wires from A battery.
- Bad rheostat (volume control). Often the volume in old battery sets was controlled by varying the filament voltage.

Problem: Tubes light but radio produces no sound.

- B voltage is missing. There may be a bad battery, bad wiring from battery, or any of the problems listed under the second problem in "Common Radio Problems."
- Open grid circuit in auto frequency tube caused by bad C battery. Check C battery voltage.

Problems of AC Receivers

Caution: There are high AC and DC voltages in these receivers. Be careful when touching the chassis.

Problem: Radio completely dead. Tubes do not light even after some time.

- Open circuit before power transformer. It might be a bad line cord, blown fuse, or a bad switch.
- Faulty power transformer.

Problem: Tubes light up but radio produces no sound.

- B voltage missing or too low. Remove rectifier tube and check high voltage winding of power transformer. If this is OK, check all parts of power supply. If these are OK, check for defective bypass condensers or some short circuit from B+ to ground.

Problem: Excessive hum.

- Filter condensers that have lost their capacity.
- Short circuit or open circuit in one-half of high voltage winding of power transformer.
- Shorted filter choke or speaker field coil.

Problem: Crackling or sputtering noise.

- Defective transformer or choke winding. The cause may be an arc between a winding and the metal of the transformer. To test, turn off receiver. Remove all tubes, including the rectifier, and turn on set. Note if arcing can be seen or a sizzling noise heard. If not, insert rectifier tube and measure voltage across each half of high voltage winding. If winding is bad, the meter will change voltage when arcing occurs. Each winding may be tested in the same way.
- Defective bleeder resistance. Arcing between windings of wire-wound resistor or across a cracked carbon resistor can cause noise. You may be able to see arc in a darkened room.

Problems of AC/DC Receivers

Caution: In many cases the chassis of one of these low-priced radios is connected to the power line directly or through a resistor and condenser. If the plug is plugged into the wall in one way, the chassis has 110 volts on it and is dangerous! If you must work on one of these with the chassis out of the case, use an AC voltmeter to check the voltage from the chassis to a reliable ground. If it reads 110 volts, reverse the plug in the wall and check again. The safest way to work on these sets is to use an isolation transformer. (See Appendix A.)

Problem: Radio dead. Tubes and pilot light do not glow.

- Heater of one or more tubes is burned out. Tube heaters are connected in a series, so none will light if one is bad.
- Switch or line cord faulty.
- Defective ballast resistor. Early AC/DC receivers have a resistor in series with the heaters. It may be a power resistor, a resistance tube looking much like a regular tube, or a special line cord with a third resistance wire built in.

Problem: Tubes light but radio does not work.

- Tube is bad.
- B+ is low or lacking throughout receiver. This shows a bad power supply. It may be a bad rectifier, filter resistors or choke, filter condenser, or shorted bypass condenser.
- There is no plate or screen-grid voltage on one tube. Most often this will show a faulty i.f. or audio transformer or a bad plate load or screen resistor.

Problem: Pilot lamp does not light but receiver works.

- Bad pilot light. Replace with one with the correct number.
- Bad pilot lamp socket.

Output and Speaker Problems

Problem: No sound although tubes light and B voltage is normal.

- Fault in speaker. Try another speaker. Any p.m. speaker can be used to test another p.m. or field coil speaker. If testing a field coil speaker, leave the field coil connected to the old speaker but shift the voice coil wires. If the new speaker works, check voice coil leads carefully. Test voice coil with ohmmeter. It should have a low but measurable resistance (½ to 2 ohms). If the set is on and the field coil has electrical power, you will hear a click when you touch the voice coil terminals with your ohmmeter leads if the speaker is good.
- Open primary on output transformer. This will show as no plate voltage on output audio tube.
- Open or shorted secondary on output transformer. If winding is open it will have high resistance with speaker disconnected. If it is shorted, it will probably allow some sound through. A good output transformer will have a primary resistance of several hundred ohms and a secondary resistance of about one ohm.
- Tone condenser shorted. This will show as low or no voltage on the plate of the output amplifier tube.

Problem: Weak volume.

- Shorted or open field coil. Test with ohmmeter with set off. Coil should be several hundred ohms. Test pull of magnet at center of speaker with set on as in figure 28. Pull of magnet should be strong. Test with another speaker, following the procedure above for faulty speakers.

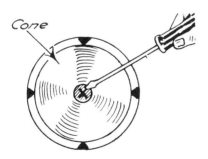

28. Testing loudspeaker magnet strength.

- Weak permanent magnet speaker magnet. Test with screwdriver as above. Try another speaker.
- Partially open voice coil. Try another speaker. Test with ohmmeter.

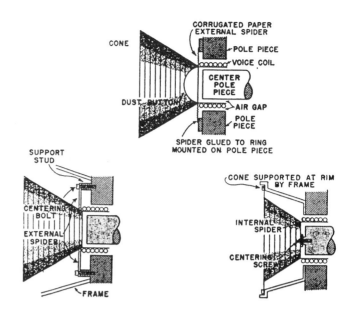

29. Centering cone of loudspeaker.

Problem: Raspy sounds.

- Metal filings or debris in gap where voice coil moves. Blow this out or try to push it out with thin paper.
- Cone warped and off center. See figure 29 for methods of mounting. Try recentering, and if you cannot, recone the speaker.

Problem: Rattling sounds.

- Loose cone or center mount. glue or tape.
- Cone warped and off center. See above.

Stage and Part Testing and Repair

Unless you are testing for voltages, all work in the chassis should be done with the power off. No soldering or resistance checking should be done with power on. Test components should be added to a set with power off. The only exception to the power-off rule is when you parallel a condenser or resistor that may be open with a good one, and you can touch the wires from the test unit to the wire leads on the one to be checked without touching either lead. (Holding the insulated body of the part is okay.) Having the set powered up in this case allows you to hear the difference the new part makes. Before doing a resistance check on a part that may be faulty, disconnect all wires going to the unit except to prevent false readings.

The problem of finding replacements is a test of patience. Appendix C lists some sources of parts and circuit information. In addition, Appendix D suggests useful repair books and pamphlets.

35

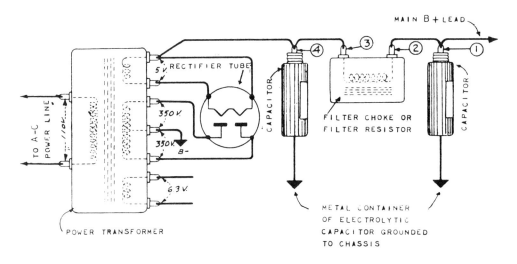

MAIN B + LEAD

RECTIFIER TUBE

CAPACITOR

FILTER CHOKE OR FILTER RESISTOR

CAPACITOR

TO A-C POWER LINE

POWER TRANSFORMER

METAL CONTAINER OF ELECTROLYTIC CAPACITOR GROUNDED TO CHASSIS

30. Typical AC power supply.

Testing Power Supplies

See figure 30 for the circuit diagram of a typical AC power supply. Other power supplies will be similar, and the AC/DC supply will have many of the same difficulties.

Alternating current from the home power line is transformed by the power transformer into the necessary high voltage AC for the rectifier, the low voltage to operate the filament of that rectifier, and the voltage necessary for the filaments of the other tubes in the set. By taping the high voltage winding of the power transformer at the center and grounding that center for B-, the alternating current in the high voltage coil will switch back and forth from +350 volts at the top and -350 volts at the bottom to -350 at the top and +350 at the bottom. Since the rectifier has two plates connected to opposite ends of the winding, one plate will always be positive with respect to the filament of the rectifier and will draw current, whereas the other, being negative, will not. Thus, one plate will be drawing current at all times. The current drawn from the filament will cause the filament of the rectifier to appear positive, for it will have a shortage of electrons with respect to the center tap, which is B-.

We now have an electrical current traveling in one direction, since the filament will always be positive. We have obtained DC from AC, but the DC is not even. It has a ripple corresponding to the waveform of the original AC, as can be seen in figure 31. This ripple will sound like a 120 hertz hum in the receiver. To eliminate it, a filter consisting of two electrolytic condensers and a filter choke is added.

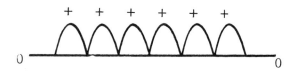

31. Power supply ripple (DC).

This filter resists variations in the DC applied to it, averages the variations, and gives a smooth output to the B+ lead. Some power supplies will use a resistor and higher capacity condensers instead. Often several condensers are contained in the same case or can.

If the B voltages throughout the radio seem to be low, you need to decide if the problem is in the power supply, or if the radio, because of some fault, is demanding more power than the supply can give.

To make that decision, look at a more obvious problem. If there is a noticeable hum in the receiver, you probably have a problem with one of the filter condensers. Sometimes a condenser will not only lose its capacity to filter, but will also develop an internal partial short circuit and draw too much power. If one of the condensers becomes warm to the touch, this is likely to be the problem. Test by substituting a good condenser. If the voltages are okay, but the hum persists, simply place the new condenser in parallel with the old.

When you replace a filter condenser, remember that high voltage exists on its positive (+) connection. Remember, also, to wire the test condenser with the same polarity (+ to + and - to -). If you wire an electrolytic condenser backwards it will be destroyed immediately. Checking the filters will cure many low voltage and hum problems. Do remember that your test or replacement condenser should have the same or higher capacity and the same or higher working voltage.

A difficult problem to spot is the power supply that will not provide high enough voltage to the set for it to operate properly. It is sometimes hard to know what the voltage should be for the set without a circuit diagram, but it should be over 100 volts in an AC set, more than likely in the range of 250 volts.

If the set is not working well and low voltage seems to be present at the second filter condenser (point 1 in figure 30), you need to discover if the problem is in the power supply or in the radio itself. Do this by measuring the voltage at point

1 and writing it down. Turn off the radio and discharge the condensers by short circuiting point 1 to ground. Disconnect the main B+ wire to the radio and turn on the power supply. The voltage at point 1 should now be higher than before, but not by more than about 30 percent. If the voltage at this point rises sharply, then something in the radio itself is drawing too much current for the power supply to provide.

If the voltage at point 1 does not rise much and still seems to be too low, for example under 200 volts for an AC supply using a power transformer, you have a weak power supply. One cause may be a poor rectifier tube. After a long period of use, rectifiers will lose the ability to pass enough electrons to supply sufficient current. The only repair is replacement of the tube. If the voltage of the supply seems low when the B+ lead is reconnected to the rest of the radio, check the voltage at point 4 in figure 30 and compare it with that at point 1. If your power supply uses a filter choke (a large metal case looking like a transformer), there should be no more than a 15 to 30 volt drop across it. If the drop is high, 60 or more volts, either your receiver is drawing too much current or you have a bad filter choke. If the voltage drop is very low from point 4 to 1 and the overall voltage to the set is low, the rectifier tube is likely to be at fault.

And what if there is no high voltage at all? If you get nothing at point 1, check to see if there is anything at point 4. If nothing is there, remove the rectifier tube and measure the AC voltage at the plate pins on the socket. Measure each side to the center tap. The two voltages should be within 10 percent of each other and should be somewhere from 125 to 350 volts AC. If there is no voltage here, check to see if tubes are lit. If they are, there is trouble in the power transformer. If they are not lit, there may be transformer trouble or a problem in the wiring preceding it. Resistance testing, with the plug pulled, should help you find the problem.

You can check the voltage at each winding of the power transformer. If only one is missing, there is a fault in the power transformer. Direct replacements are hard to find but the fault may not be too bad. Find where the wires go into the transformer. Sometimes they will connect to a metal terminal and break at that point. If there is no break, the transformer may need to be rewound, which is no job for a beginner. If you suspect a faulty transformer, disconnect the suspected winding completely and check it with the ohmmeter of your multitester. Figure 32 shows the average DC resistance in a good transformer. If the resistance is

much higher, for example, ten times higher, you probably have a bad winding. If a power transformer is bad, a new unit can be substituted if you know the rating of the old one, but the authenticity of your set will suffer. It is better to have the old one rewound or find a direct replacement.

Filter chokes can also develop an open winding, since a filter choke is really a transformer with a single winding. If you suspect this, disconnect one lead and measure the resistance. It should be somewhere between 15 and 250 ohms. If voltage drops across it when the supply is running, check the resistance—with power off, of course! It is a good idea to check the resistance of transformer and choke windings to ground as well. Center taps on power transformer windings that are connected to ground will have to be disconnected, of course. With the winding completely disconnected, the resistance to ground should be so high as to be almost unmeasurable. A faulty filter choke can be replaced with a power resistor of at least 5 watt power capacity and about 500 ohms of resistance. Chokes can be rewound, like transformers.

33. Selenium rectifier.

Some receivers have a selenium rectifier (figure 33). These were usually used in battery, AC/DC portables. Problems with selenium rectifiers show up as excessive hum or no B+. They cannot be fixed, but can be replaced with modern silicon diodes of at least 400 volt peak inverse voltage rating and 1 amp capacity. Power supplies are usually quite reliable. It is more likely that trouble will arise from rectifier tubes and filter condensers.

Electrolytic Condenser Testing

These condensers appear in power supplies, and they are also used in many sets to bypass audio voltages around a resistor and to further smooth B+ between stages in the set, making oscillation less likely.

The best test for an electrolytic is replacement, but they can also be tested with an ohmmeter. Disconnect the + lead with the set off. Touch the black test lead from the meter to the ground (-) side, and touch the red lead to the + side. The meter will swing sharply towards the 0 end of the dial, then climb until it reads a high resistance. Several hundred thousand ohms is good. If the resistance remains low, the condenser is leaky. If the meter does not move at all when you touch the red lead to +, the condenser is open. In either case, replace it.

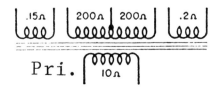

32. Power transformer DC resistance.

Transformer and Choke Testing

Some suggestions for testing are given above in the section on power supplies. Figures 32 and 34 show the resistances in good transformers. Remember to test for short

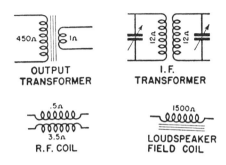

34. Transformer DC resistances.

circuits to the case of the transformer with all wires to the windings disconnected. The same sort of tests can be carried out on r.f. transformers. Faults will be more likely to appear in the primary winding of r.f. and a.f. transformers than in the secondary winding, because the primary has high voltage and high current flow. Any radio part subjected to high current and high voltage is more vulnerable to failure.

If something seems to be wrong with any transformer, check the emerging wires for shorts to cases or breaks. To solder a wire coming from a transformer, scrape it clean first. It may look shiny, but it is covered with an insulating varnish that must be removed before solder will adhere.

When checking transformers using the resistances in figures 32 and 34, remember that these are only approximate resistances. A circuit diagram for your specific set may give accurate DC resistances. A transformer's resistances may vary a couple of times over from the suggested ones and the part still be good.

Tuning Condenser Testing and Repair

If you have carefully cleaned the tuning condenser, the largest problem remaining is slightly bent plates that cause a short circuit. If the condenser works over only part of the dial, a short is to be suspected. If you can see nothing touching, disconnect the wire from the stators, the fixed plates that are usually insulated from the frame. Connect an ohmmeter between the stators and the rotors, the moving plates, which are usually grounded. Rotate the rotor of the condenser slowly from one end to the other. The resistance should be unmeasurably high all the time. Watch the meter as you turn the plates. If the resistance drops sharply, something is shorting the plates. Examine them carefully while shorted, using a good light. You should be able to see the point at which they touch. Clean that point or bend the touching rotating plate carefully. With careful touch and patience, you should be able to fix nearly any tuning condenser.

Another problem with tuning condensers is the breaking or corroding of the spring or wire that connects the rotor with the frame. (See figure 15.) This will result in poor contact between the rotor and the frame, which leads to erratic operation. If a wire or spring is broken, fix it with a piece of stranded wire long enough to allow the condenser to rotate over its normal 180° range. Use cleaner and fine sandpaper on a corroded contact. Your ohmmeter can tell you if there is a problem here. There should be zero resistance between the rotor and the frame.

Trimmer and Paper Condenser Testing and Repair

Trimmer condensers, with their mica dielectric, will seldom cause problems. If trouble is suspected, they are tested in the same way as variable condensers. Usually the only repair needed will be cleaning.

Paper condensers are far more troublesome. The oiled paper dielectric was not very good to begin with and age takes a further toll. These condensers, when subjected to high voltages as in bypass, coupling, or tone duty, are vulnerable. There is no way to fix them. For authenticity's sake, open the case of the bad unit and put a modern capacitor inside. Since the modern unit is generally smaller, this can be done.

With a paper condenser, the beeswax can be melted out in a low-temperature oven and saved. Place a new capacitor of the same capacity and equal or higher working voltage in the tube, leaving wires sticking out the ends, and pour wax into the tube.

Other units that are mounted in plastic boxes will sometimes be sealed with a black substance that can be melted out, although this is a messy job. Some units are in metal cans that can be unsoldered and opened.

The best test for a suspected paper condenser is to replace it in the circuit and see if the new one works. It can also be tested with an ohmmeter, following the procedure for testing an electrolytic. Set the ohmmeter to its highest resistance setting. Connect one test lead to one side and, while watching the meter carefully, touch the other lead to the other condenser wire. The meter will move a little at first but should settle at a resistance of not less than 700,000 ohms. If the meter needle does not move at all, the condenser is probably open. If the resistance is lower than it should be, it is leaky and should be replaced. Again, remember that condenser tests are made with one wire from the condenser disconnected from the radio circuit.

Resistor Testing and Repair

Carbon resistors can change resistance value, especially when they carry much current. Resistances should be within + or -10 percent of the marked value, although a variation of 20 percent is often acceptable. Test resistors with an ohmmeter and with one end of the resistor disconnected. Grid leak resistors have a resistance of 5 to 10 million ohms and only the best meters will measure them. The most successful way to check them is to replace them. If a grid leak tube has an excessively high negative grid voltage and will not work at all, the resistor is probably open. Carbon resistors cannot be repaired. They should be replaced with a resistor within 10 percent of the original value and of equal or greater power capacity. Use the color code chart in figure 21 to learn the value of a resistor.

Wire-wound resistors can suffer corrosion, burnout, or broken leads. If a lead burns off at one end, you may be able to unwind one loop and gain enough length to refasten it. If you should find a resistor of any kind badly burned, try to isolate what draws current through it and thus overloaded it. Resistors don't burn by themselves. Check any associated bypass condensers for short circuits.

Volume Control Repair

Volume controls can be cleaned and, on occasion, wirewound types can be rewound or soldered. Beyond that, not much can be done with them. If a control works but makes a little noise when it is rotated, that is not great problem. If you replace a volume control, remember that the resistance is important and so is the taper, the amount of resistance change for a given rotation of the knob. Volume controls

that act on the antenna circuit or the grid circuit of an audio tube are usually audio taper. Controls that affect the tube filament voltage are linear. Tone controls are usually linear. You can switch around the types of tapers, but if you do, operation will not be as good.

Controls are cleaned, as mentioned earlier, by generously spraying TV tuner-cleaner into them and rotating the shaft to move the wiping element of the control back and forth. Sometimes the moving wiper in the control can be bent a little to make better contact as well.

Tube Testing and Replacement

Since vacuum tubes are the most common cause of trouble in radios, lack of a tube tester makes it hard to do an efficient repair job. Tubes are available but costly and you do not want to replace any that aren't bad. A careful troubleshooting job can often determine if a particular tube needs replacement. If one tube has a filament that does not light when the others do, it probably has burned out. Even if the filament lights, it may have lost the ability to supply enough electrons to operate well. Something inside the tube may have come loose, and the tube will develop an internal

Stromberg Carlson, model 636A, 1928, AC, neutrodyne. Photographed at St. Louis Museum of Science and Natural History.

Majestic, model 71, 1928, AC. Photographed at Western Heritage Museum.

short circuit. If you are suspicious of a tube, check its filament with an ohmmeter. Some battery tubes have filaments so thin that they are nearly impossible to see even when lit.

You may be able to get tubes tested at a radio shop. Even if they are old four-, five-, six-, and seven-pin types, a radio shop run by an older man may have an old-style tube tester. Later eight-pin (octal) and most small miniature tubes can be tested at any radio-TV shop or Radio Shack store that has do-it-yourself tube testers. If you know radio amateurs in your area, they may be able to help with tube checking and other problems.

Appendix B gives some of the more common tube base layouts and information about those tubes. For more information, consult one of the reprint tube manuals or repair books listed in Appendix D.

Metal Castings Repair

Many early sets used pot metal castings for switches, variable condenser frames, and even chassis. Deterioration caused by time and poor casting technique often leads to breaking, warping, or flaking of the metal. While it may be possible to recast simple pieces, repair is more desirable. We've found that epoxy cement glues pot metal well. Pieces may be joined and badly flaking or warping pieces stabilized and rescued by flowing epoxy into the cracks or building up thin spots. This method isn't elegant, but it works and may, in many cases, be the only repair available.

Atwater Kent, model 55, 1929, AC,TRF. Photographed at Museum of Wonderful Wireless.

Atwater Kent, model 52, AC, TRF, metal cabinet. Photographed at Western Heritage Museum.

Atwater Kent display. Photographed at Museum of Wonderful Wireless.

RCA Victor, model RE-45, 1929, AC, TRF, radio-phonograph, doors open.

RCA Victor, model RE-45, 1929, AC, TRF, radio-phonograph, doors closed.

Atwater Kent, 55C chassis (restored), 1929, TRF.

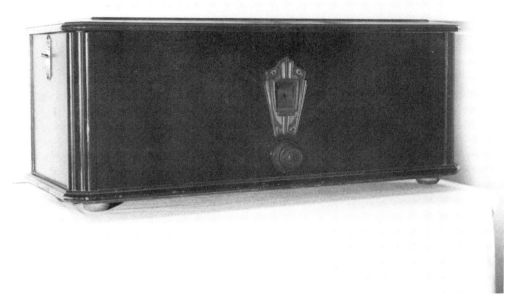

RCA, Radiola 44, 1929, AC, TRF.

Atwater Kent, model 55, 1929, AC, TRF, unrestored cabinet, doors open.

Atwater Kent, model 55, 1929, AC, TRF, unrestored cabinet, doors closed.

7 Fine-tuning Your Radio

You want your receiver to work the best it possibly can. This may require aligning or touching up the adjustment of the internal controls. You'll need an adequate antenna and ground. Most old sets used an outside antenna, unlike our sensitive modern radios with their loop antennas or loopsticks.

Any adjustment of the trimmer condensers on the chassis or on the tuning condensers should be done with great care. It is easy to make things worse than they are. A safe rule for any person who does not have an r.f. signal generator is this: "If it works satisfactorily, leave it alone." Your set may not be at peak efficiency, but it may be good enough. No harm is done by not having it perfectly aligned.

On a superheterodyne receiver, alignment must be especially carefully done. Follow the instructions that came with the signal generator and also the alignment instructions for your particular radio.

Lacking a generator, there are a number of adjustments you can make. You will need a screwdriver with an insulated tip or, if your receiver needs it, a plastic hex wrench to adjust trimmers and i.f. transformers. Alignment tool sets are inexpensive and helpful.

The basic rule is to start with the adjustments closest to the speaker. Refer to figure 37 for a typical superhet. Begin by tuning in a fairly weak station. Keep the volume of your set just loud enough to hear. Start with the secondary of T-2, which is on the side facing the detector and output tubes. Turn the screw adjustment here one-half turn. Is the received station louder? If so, turn the screw further until the sound begins to get softer. If the sound grew softer when you initially turned the screw, return screw to the original position and back a half-turn the other way. Find the maximum output. Whenever you turn a trimmer control, turn it only a small distance each time. If adjusting the control seems to make no noticeable difference, put it back where it was originally.

Once you have adjusted the secondary of T-2, adjust its primary in the same way. Then move back to T-1, adjusting secondary first and then primary. If the station starts getting very loud as you adjust, tune down the volume. It is easier to hear changes at low volume.

After tuning the i.f. transformers, T-1, and T-2, proceed to the r.f. tuning trimmer (C-8), which is sometimes called the antenna trimmer. After that, find a station near the bottom of the dial, as close to 600 kH. as possible, to touch up the oscillator trimmer. If reception is good before you touch the oscillator trimmer, stop. Changing the oscillator frequency spacing can be a problem. If you try, don't forget the original setting.

In any adjustment, turn the screw one-half turn one way. If that increases volume, keep turning slowly. If it decreases the volume, turn it back, and try the other direction. If you lose reception or hear a squeal, your stage has gone into oscillation, which it should not do. Something is wrong. You can back off the adjustment, but it is better to examine the stage to which the i.f. transformer is connected and try to correct the problem. Tubes are often at fault here.

On tuned radio frequency receivers (TRF), each r.f. section must be tuned to be in line with the other. TRF receivers have a tendency to be more sensitive at one end of the dial than the other, so it is best if you work in the middle or toward the less sensitive end. If you have no signal generator, find a station near the middle. Keep the volume fairly low. Start at the end closest to the detector and tune the trimmer that is associated with that section of the multisection condenser. Try turning it one-half turn one way, then the other. Set it for maximum loudness of the station. Check by working back towards the antenna. You want the loudest volume without oscillation.

In some sets, no adjustments can be made. Obviously, those sets cannot be fine-tuned. In any alignment job, it is good to go back to the beginning and do it over after you have finished, making smaller adjustments this time.

Antenna Systems

See figure 35 for a possible antenna arrangement. Old sets without loop antennas need a substantial antenna system. In general, the higher and longer the antenna, the better. But before you put up an outside antenna, experiment a little. A ground connection to a water pipe and a piece of wire stretched near the ceiling of a room may suffice as an antenna for local stations.

If you are serious about listening, though, you will want an outside antenna. Radio Shack stores sell an antenna package they call a "short wave" antenna that is quite satisfactory. They also sell a grounding rod that can be used for an outside ground connection. We have our ground rod located near a downspout drain where the ground stays moist.

Antenna systems can attract lightning, so it is best to

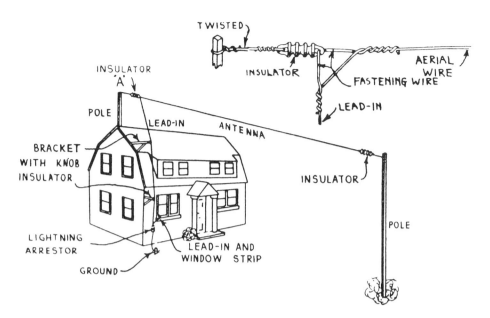

35. Typical outside antenna.

have them grounded when not in use. A lightning arrestor may be placed between the antenna and its ground, but it is still a good idea to locate a knife-switch inside the window connecting the antenna and ground. When the switch is closed, the antenna will have a direct connection to ground. The only time we leave our antenna ungrounded is when it is actually being used. Never use an outside antenna during an electrical storm. Reception will be poor, and the situation can be dangerous.

You may need to ground your receiver as well. Older battery receivers will almost always need to be grounded for good results. AC/DC receivers should never be grounded. AC receivers with power transformers may or may not work better with a ground. Try it both ways.

Using and Maintaining Your Radio

You fixed that antique radio in order to use it. Still, remember that your old radio, like an antique car, is not up to heavy, day-in-and-day-out use. Old tubes and old parts will fail in time. They can be replaced or fixed, but repairs can be difficult and expensive.

Remember, too, that your old radio will usually not be as sensitive or sound as good as a modern set does, partly because of its age and partly because the newer sets use improved technology. It is good, though, to use your old radio regularly. Filter condensers will stay in better shape, controls will not get stiff or "freeze" on their shafts, and you will spot problems early, when they can be fixed easily. An hour or so a week of use will help keep your radio healthy. (It is nice to be able to brag a little, too: "I was listening to Chicago last night on my fifty-year-old radio, and. . . . ")

Keep it clean, too. Old wooden cabinets respond to polishing with a soft cloth and lemon oil. Paste wax works well on plastic cabinets. Every couple of years, you may want to

take the chassis out of its case and clean it again as you did when you brought it home.

Use your radio with sense, take care of it, and get to know its personality. You are preserving a valuable piece of electrical history. It probably won't make you rich, but it will give you a lot of satisfaction.

Northland, serial number 6831, table radio. Photographed at Museum of Wonderful Wireless.

44

A.C. Dayton, AC-9970, 1929, AC, TRF, doors closed.

A.C. Dayton, AC-9970, 1929, AC, TRF, doors open.

Kolster 45, 1929, remote control console. Photographed at St. Louis Museum of Science and Natural History.

Kolster 45. Remote control unit resembles this side panel and is connected to the radio by wire.

KOLSTER SPEAKER

Equipped with a highly sensitive oversize magnet and a driving unit that is one of the finest, the Kolster responds instantly to the faintest impulse. It faithfully reproduces both voice and orchestra from the faintest whisper to the fullest volume of a brass band.

Dimensions: Height, 11 inches; width, 11 inches; depth, 6½ inches.

LIST PRICE, $35.00

Our Price $4.50

Kolster speaker advertisement, 1931.

Philmore, crystal set. Photographed at St. Louis Museum of Science and Natural History.

Kennedy shortwave converter, model 53. Photographed at Museum of Wonderful Wireless.

8 Cabinet Repairing and Refinishing

Always begin by cleaning your radio cabinet with turpentine or mineral spirits and 3/0 steel wool. Even if you are going to strip the finish later, it is good to get the old wax and dirt off. Use of 3/0 steel wool reduces the possibility of scratching the finish, but you still must be careful. Leaning too heavily on the steel wool results in scratches where your fingers pushed against the wood. Work a square foot at a time with the turpentine and steel wool, then collect the residue with a clean soft cloth. Do the edges of the wood as well as the flat parts, and remove knobs to clean the wood under them.

If the radio has a good but dull finish, go no further. Lemon oil and a soft cloth will polish away the dullness. Polish small areas, since it is necessary to remove excess oil before it gets sticky or attracts dust. Do not use lemon oil and wax combinations because these will start the wax buildup. In time the wax may darken, changing the color of the radio cabinet.

Using Refinishers

If the finish is bad, you may decide to refinish the cabinet. If so, use a refinishing product rather than a stripper. (In some cases stripping may be necessary. More about that later.) A refinisher will take more work than a stripper, but it is easier on the wood. Take the chassis out of the cabinet, of course, keeping all knobs, screws, and other loose parts with the chassis. Label parts to avoid confusion later.

There are many brands of refinishers in hardware stores. People may prefer Formby's, Hope's, or White's, which are all commonly available. Probably more brands are being added all the time. Follow the directions that come with the refinisher you buy.

There are, however, general rules that apply to most, if not all, of these products. Use them in shade to avoid the sun's too rapid evaporation of their solvents. Don't use them in drafts because wind evaporates solvents, also. Don't use in temperatures below 65° F. because cold slows their ability to work. Use them with adequate ventilation, for their fumes can be poisonous. If you use them inside, open windows and also provide for cross ventilation. Since you should not use them in drafts, put yourself in the draft and your work just outside it.

Pour about two cups of refinisher into a metal or glass container. Cap the refinisher immediately. Divide a pad of 3/0 steel wool into three or four pieces and put on rubber gloves. Wet the steel wool in the refinisher, squeezing it until it is damp but not dripping. Apply to an area the size of a plate on the top of the cabinet. Work in a circular pattern. When the finish starts melting and the pad begins to gum up, rinse the pad in the refinisher and start the area again. You can continue to do this until the refinisher becomes thick and sludgy. (Refinisher is expensive, and you can reclaim some of it by pouring the dirty refinisher into a tightly covered jar. When the residue settles to the bottom, pour off the clean refinisher and use it again.)

When one area is clean wood, move on to another area, remembering to overlap the previous area. When the entire cabinet is clean, take some fresh refinisher and a clean pad and go over it again to remove any remaining finish. Allow the cabinet to dry for an hour. Buff the entire surface lightly but thoroughly with clean steel wool. The surface will now be ready for its new finish.

Using Strippers

If the radio has been painted, a paint stripper is better and easier to use than a refinisher. There are even more opinions about which paint stripper to use than there are about refinishers. Talk to those who use them or to a trusted hardware salesperson and follow their recommendation until you gain experience and form your own preference. There are water based strippers, nonwater based strippers, thick strippers, and thin strippers. Follow the directions on the can carefully. The various kinds of strippers have different directions, but we can give some general rules that apply to most.

Do not use indoors. Do not use in the sun. Do not use when the temperature is below 65° F. (Some strippers shouldn't be used in temperatures above 90° F.). Always wear rubber gloves and old clothes. Lay on the stripper thickly in one direction on a small section.

Be careful when using putty knives to remove stripper. It is very easy to gouge the wood with a corner of the putty knife. If you're using one, round the corners of the knife first. Toothbrushes are excellent for getting into corners and around carvings. Give the stripper enough time to operate to avoid doing the job again.

After the stripper is removed, go over the entire cabinet with mineral spirits or turpentine to remove any residue.

Interesting cabinet, manufacturer unknown, ca. 1930. Photographed at Western Heritage Museum.

Brunswick, model 15, 1930, AC. Photographed at Western Heritage Museum.

Staining and Varnishing

Once the cabinet is down to bare wood, the choice of stains, fillers, and varnishes is yours. Again, whatever you use, follow the directions carefully.

If you wish to fill the grain so the surface is flat and smooth, buy paste wood filler in walnut, mahogany, or a natural color. Having the color mixed into the filler makes the finishing much easier. Some people skip this step completely, relying on their varnish to smooth the surface.

In most cases you will want to stain the cabinet. This will even the color of the wood, which is a good idea since manufacturers often used many different woods. Stains may be water or oil based, runny or gelled. Probably the easiest to use and the most forgiving is gelled stain or pigmented wiping stain. Follow the can directions exactly. In most cases you rub on these stains with 3/0 steel wool. Many people use soft, lintless rags, such as diapers or T-shirts, but these rags may wick some of the pigment from the stain and leave a less uniform color over the surface. Use a stain darker than the result you want. Wipe it on, let it remain for ten to

fifteen minutes, then gently wipe off the remaining stain with a soft, lintless rag. You may wipe off as much as you wish and thus control how dark the finish will be. After using a gelled stain, wait seventy-two hours before applying a finish coat.

Sometimes the stain color looks artificially flat, with too little variation. The simplest way of correcting this is to wipe on a darker stain, such as walnut over oak or mahogany, and immediately wipe it off across the grain. A bit of the darker stain remains in the grain of the wood, and the whole piece takes on a more genuine look. To darken the entire piece slightly, use a colored varnish for your first wipe-on coat.

Most old wooden radios were varnished. Ready your cabinet for varnishing by sanding with a fine sandpaper (140-180) with the grain. If it is impossible to sand with the grain, such as in areas around carving or over parquetry, use a very light touch on the sandpaper. Finish with extra-fine sandpaper (220-280). If the wood is very smooth, use a wipe-on varnish. If the finish still has a visible grain, even the surface by using varnish applied with a brush.

Philco, model 90, 1931, AC. Photographed at Western Heritage Museum.

Philco, model 50, 1931, TRF.

A wipe-on varnish finish is applied with a cloth rather than a paintbrush. Use a satin varnish. If you are using varnish to change the color of the stain, for instance, using walnut varnish to slightly mellow red mahogany, wipe on the first coats even if you use a brush for the final varnish coats.

Before applying varnish, wipe the entire cabinet with a tack rag or a lintless cloth dampened with mineral spirts or turpentine. Wait for the turpentine to dry. Cut a piece of cloth large enough to make a comfortable pad in your hand. Pour some of the varnish into a pan (aluminum pot-pie pans are excellent) and cover the varnish can immediately. Dampen the rag in the varnish and wipe it over a small area on the surface of the wood. Work from the top to the bottom of the cabinet as you did when you stripped it. When you complete wiping on the varnish, use the same cloth to wipe off excess varnish in the direction of the grain. There should be no wet-looking spots. Continue until the cabinet is finished. Let it dry overnight, then sand lightly with extra-fine sandpaper, and reapply varnish. It may take five to ten coats to build a finish. It takes time, but it is easy to do.

If varnish is being applied with a brush, air bubbles can be a problem. For this reason, do not paint back and forth with the brush. Starting with one edge, apply two brush widths of varnish across the grain. Then spread the varnish across the width of another stroke. This spreads the finish in the direction of the grain. Continue to work across the piece, always allowing one space and two varnish-filled brush widths. This way you can do the final brushing with

the grain of the wood and working into the section you have just finished. Always finish a section by lightly using the tips of the bristles, brushing the section just completed into the previously finished section. This will keep one section from being thicker than another.

When the varnish is dry, lightly sand the surface and dust it again with a tack rag. Apply another coat. Usually two coats are enough.

If a satin finish is shinier than you want, you can dull it without loosing any of the character of the wood. In fact, using pumice and rottenstone makes it possible to produce a matte finish with great depth. This takes some work, but the results are spectacular.

You'll need pumice, rottenstone, rubbing oil, and a felt pad. Your hardware store may have these; otherwise they're available from the Woodworkers' Store (See Appendix C). The rubbing felt spreads the weight of your fingers and prevents uneven rubbing. Spread rubbing oil lightly on the piece, sprinkle with pumice, and rub lightly with the felt pad. Add oil on the surface when the pad begins dragging instead of sliding. Rub lightly and evenly. When you finish with the pumice, the surface will look scratched. Take the rottenstone, which is even finer than pumice, and go through the entire process again to produce a deep, non-glossy finish. Remove the remaining oil with a clean rag and a bit of fresh rubbing oil.

No matter how you finish your cabinet, end with a polish of pure lemon oil.

Veneer Replacement

Veneer should be replaced before you refinish the cabinet after staining. Replacing veneer is a cut-and-try project. Trim out the rough veneer around the missing piece with a sharp knife, making a smooth-edged pattern that can be transferred to your replacement veneer later. Match stains, being sure to stain a large enough piece of veneer so that you can cut several pieces if you need to in order to get a good fit.

Straight edges are easier to match than curved ones, but you don't want to make a perfect square or the join will be obvious. Angled lines are easier to overlook, so parallelograms, trapezoids, and other angled patches are best. Lay a piece of thin paper over the missing veneer and, as carefully as you can, trace around it with a sharp pencil. Cut this pattern and lay it in the hole to see where it is wrong. If your pattern is too large, trim it down to size. If it's too small, make another larger one. Cut and try until you have a good fit. It's easier to experiment on paper than on veneer.

Cut the veneer, remembering to keep the grains going in the same direction and to match the style of grain as closely as possible. If you're lucky, the piece of veneer will fit on the first try. If it doesn't, trim it or cut another, slightly larger, piece.

Use white glue to install the veneer. If you have clamps or straps, use them. It's important to snug the veneer tightly to get a flush top surface with no cracks around the replacement. If you don't have clamps, make simple ones using two books, plastic wrap, and some strong cord. Lay the plastic wrap over the veneer, making sure no glue is seeping out, hold a book over the patch, put the other book on the opposite side of the cabinet, and have someone else pull the cord tightly around the entire project and tie a firm knot. This should apply pressure on the patch, while preventing the cord from digging into the wood on the other side of the radio. Leave overnight before unfastening.

Philco, model 38, 1933, battery. Photographed at Western Heritage Museum.

Grille Cloth Repair

If grille cloth is in good condition, you're lucky. Leave it alone.

If it is very thin and showing bad wear or rips, repair the original cloth if possible. Using a neutral-colored silk, make a sandwich of grille cloth (front side down), "Stitch Witchery" or some other interfacing that fuses two pieces of fabric together, and silk. Be sure there are no wrinkles. If there are loose threads in the speaker cloth, place them as smoothly parallel as possible. Follow the directions for the fusible interfacing. Most directions require that you set your iron at wool, use a damp press cloth, and press with a stationary iron on each area for ten seconds. When cool, the sandwich can be placed in the radio and will look like new. Sound transfer will be reduced slightly but not seriously.

If the grille cloth is hopeless or missing, replace it with an earthtone silk. The problem with most silks is that they are colored with intense dyes. An old radio calls for something that looks more antique. If you can find any threads of the original grille cloth still in the radio try to match their color. Getting suitably patterned grille cloth is probably impossible, although you might find a modern brocade that will substitute well. Plain silk is at least neutral enough not to clash with the radio. Sound can travel through it without being muffled as might happen with some tighter weave fabrics.

Diamond, table radio. Photographed at Museum of Wonderful Wireless.

Kennedy Coronet, model 42, 1931-32, TRF. Photographed at Museum of Wonderful Wireless.

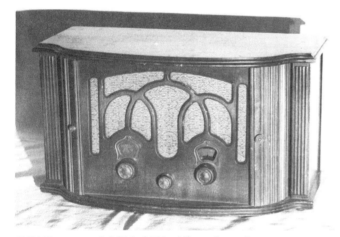

RCA Victor, model 28D, 1933, AC, tambour doors open.

Philco, model 91, ("Baby Grand"), 1932, AC. Photographed at Western Heritage Museum.

RCA Victor, model 28D, 1933, AC, tambour doors closed. Photographed at Museum of Wonderful Wireless.

Philco, model 44, AC. Photographed at Western Heritage Museum.

Erla, model 271, AC, TRF. Photographed at Museum of Wonderful Wireless.

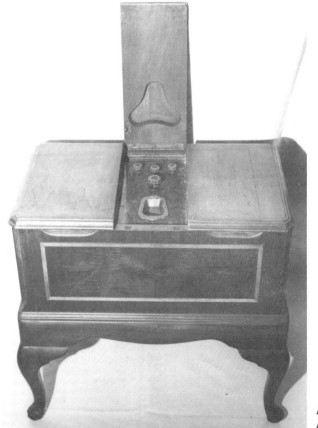

Philco, model 14, 1933, chairside model closed.

Philco, model 14, 1933, chairside model open. Photographed at Heritage Museum.

RCA Radiola advertising scarf used in showroom.

RCA Victor, model 143, 1933. Photographed at Museum of Wonderful Wireless.

General Electric, model K-43, 1934. Photographed at Western Heritage Museum.

RCA Victor, model 140, 1934. Photographed at Museum of Wonderful Wireless.

9 Receiver Theory

This chapter will detail the operation of three common types of receivers. The superheterodyne, being the most common, will be covered first, even though it is the most complex. The tuned radio frequency and regenerative circuits used in older sets will be examined as well. While this chapter is not essential for the use of the tips and guidelines in the rest of this book, it will help you to understand the working of circuit components. You may want to read more of radio theory as well.

Superheterodyne Receivers

See a typical superheterodyne circuit from the early 1940s in figures 36, 37, and 38. In the power circuits, the filaments of the five tubes are connected in series across the power line. Notice that the filament voltages, expressed in the first tube number, are 12, 12, 12, 35, and 50, which add up to 121. Since this is close to the 115 volts the line supplies, the filaments can be series connected across the AC line without an extra resistance.

The B voltage is obtained from the 35Z5 rectifier. AC is applied to the plate of the 35Z5 through part of the 35Z5 filament, the pilot light, and R-7, which gives surge protection. Rectified B+ is obtained from the cathode and is filtered by C-4, C-5, and R-8. This smooths the ripple in the DC. A higher voltage for the audio output is taken off before R-8. A slightly lower voltage for the other tubes

comes off after the filter resistor R-8. The second R-7 connected to the cathode directly acts to protect the rectifier from shorts or surges.

In the antenna circuit, the loop antenna (L-1) is also the antenna coil and is tuned by variable condenser G-1 to preselect the desired frequency. G-8 in parallel with G-1 serves to adjust the loop for best reception at the top end of the dial. An extra loop of wire couples to the loop antenna for attachment from direct connection to the chassis ground while still allowing an r.f. connection to ground.

In the converter circuit, the preselected signal from L-1 arrives at grid 3 of the 12SA7 converter tube, where it is mixed with a signal generated in the same tube in the following way.

One winding of the oscillator coil, L-1, is attached from the cathode to ground. The other winding of L-2 is attached to grid 1 of the tube. Any signal arriving at grid 1 is of such a phase in relation to the cathode that the tube will amplify its own signal and oscillate. Grids 2 and 4, which are internally connected, are fed B+ directly and are grounded, so far as any signal is concerned, through the filter condensers. Grid 2 acts as the plate for the oscillator section of the tube.

The oscillator is tuned to a frequency lower than the received frequency on grid 3 by G-2, which is in a tuned circuit with one side of L-2. Since G-2 turns on the same tuning shaft as G-1, which preselects the signal, the oscillator will change frequency with the changing of the tuning

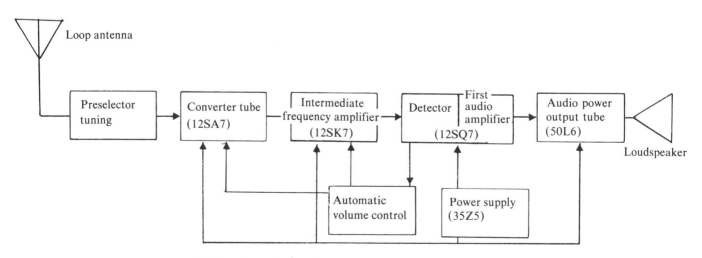

36. Typical superheterodyne receiver (functional block diagram).

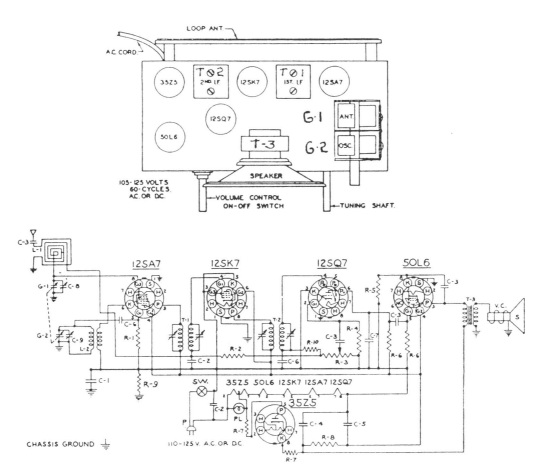

37. Typical superheterodyne receiver (chassis layout and circuit diagram).

condenser. C-9 is the trimmer adjustment used to get exactly the right oscillator frequency difference.

The difference between the desired station and the lower oscillator frequency is called the intermediate frequency, or i.f. In modern AM superheterodyne receivers the i.f. is usually 456 kH. In older superhets it is often a lower frequency. The circuit diagram of your set will usually give the i.f. frequency.

How do the two frequencies get mixed and a new one obtained? Remember that the cathode of the 12SA7 is supplying a current that varies in frequency with the oscillator. That same varying electron stream is also controlled by the preselected frequency signal on grid 3. The result is that on the plate of the 12SA7 there will be 4 frequencies. The oscillator frequency (0), the preselected program frequency (P), and also P + 0 and P - 0.

The first i.f. transformer (T-1) is tuned to P - 0, which is always the intermediate frequency. The other signals, being considerably different in frequency, are rejected.

The condensers on T-1 are used to tune its primary and secondary to the exact intermediate frequency. The 12SA7 receives its plate voltage and passes on this signal through the primary of T-1.

One more point before we leave the converter: R-1 is necessary to provide a DC return to ground for grid 1, preventing electron buildup that would eventually block the grid. The resistance provides some bias to grid 1, which is kept on the grid by blocking condenser C-6. The necessary

bias on grid 3 is obtained from the automatic volume control (AVC) circuit.

The 12SK7 is a pentode amplifier that amplifies the modulated intermediate frequency signal. Grid 1 of the i.f. amplifier receives its signal from the secondary of T-1, which has its signal circuit completed to ground through C-6 and its bias supplied by the AVC circuit of R-10, R-3, R-2, and C-2. The second, or screen grid that makes high amplification in one tube possible, receives its high voltage directly from B+. This grid greatly reduces the likelihood that the tube will oscillate by reducing its plate to grid capacity. The third, or suppressor grid, is attached directly to the grounded cathode. The suppressor drives back into the plate those electrons that are knocked loose by the high electron stream velocity in this high gain tube.

The plate of the 12SK7 receives its high voltage through the primary of i.f. transformer (T-2), which, like T-1, is tuned by trimmer condensers across its windings.

In the detector circuit, the i.f. signal, highly amplified across the secondary of T-2, is strong enough to act on the plate of one diode (pin 4) of the 12SQ7 tube. This diode becomes a rectifier, conducting when the plate end of T-2 is positive, allowing current then to flow through the T-2 secondary and from ground through R-10 and R-3. The ground circuit for this receiver is indicated by the dark line on the circuit diagram.

The amount of current drawn will depend on how much the plate of the diode goes positive. Remember that the i.f.

55

R-1	22 k ohm resistor		C-6	100 mmfd. mica condenser
R-2	3.3 meg ohm resistor		C-7	500 mmfd. mica condenser
R-3	1 meg ohm volume control		C-8	Antenna trimmer condenser
R-4	2.2 meg ohm resistor		C-9	Oscillator trimmer condenser
R-5	150 ohm resistor		G-1,2	Two gang tuning condenser
R-6	470 k ohm resistor		L-1	Loop antenna
R-7	33 ohm resistor		L-2	Oscillator coil
R-8	2200 ohm resistor		T-1	First i.f. transformer
R-9	220 k ohm resistor		T-2	Second i.f. transformer
R-10	47 k ohm resistor		T-3	Output transformer
C-1	.1 mfd. 400 v. condenser		S	PM loudspeaker
C-2	.05 mfd. 400 v. condenser		PL	No. 47 pilot light
C-3	.01 mfd. 400 v. condenser		SW	AC switch on volume control
C-4,5	40 mfd. + 20 mfd. 150 volt electrolytic condenser		P	Line cord

K=1,000   meg=1,000,000   mmfd.=1/1,000,000 mfd.

38. Parts list for typical superheterodyne receiver.

signal varies in amplitude (height or volume) with the original signal put on the carrier in the modulator at the transmitter (see fig. 10).

Thus, the current through R-10 and R-3 varies as the i.f. frequency of 456 kH. and the audio modulation. Condenser C-6 acts to take out the 456 kH. part of the signal leaving the audio across the series resistances R-10 and R-3. C-6 has too small a capacity to affect the audio portion.

The original signal has now been detected and only the original audio signal remains.

The automatic volume control (AVC) circuit begins where a wire comes from the juncture of R-10 and R-3. At this point we have an audio signal with a loudness that depends on the strength of the modulated signal of the station we have received. The stronger the station, the more negative the average signal at that point will be. That averaged signal flows slowly through the large (3.3 million ohm) resistor R-2, charging the comparatively high capacity (.1 mfd.) C-2. The charge on C-2 will depend on the average loudness of the program at the R-10, R-3 juncture.

But note where the top of C-2 goes. It is attached through loop antenna L-1 to the signal grid 3 of the mixer and through the secondary of T-1 to the i.f. amplifier grid. Thus the more negative C-2 becomes, the more negative the signal grid of the mixer and the i.f. amplifier become, and the less they will amplify. On loud stations the effect is that the radio automatically turns itself down, hence the name, automatic volume control, or AVC. The actual loudness in the speaker is, of course, controlled by the volume control, R-3.

In the first audio amplifier circuit, since the cathode of the 12SQ7 is grounded, the grid of the triode section must obtain its negative bias through the grid leak resistor, R-4. A grid leak works this way. The grid of a tube, being in the electron stream from the cathode to the plate, collects some electrons each time it becomes more positive. As the electrons accumulate, they make the grid more negative. Eventually the grid will become sufficiently negative to block the flow of electrons from cathode to plate completely. The grid

leak resistance lets the surplus electrons leak at a rate slow enough to keep the grid at the desired slightly negative potential or voltage.

The audio signal exists across the volume control, R-3, and is taped off by the slider of the control. The closer to R-10 the slider is, the louder the output. C-3 passes the audio signal to the grid of the 12SQ7 while blocking the bias on the grid, keeping it on the grid where it belongs.

The output of the amplifier is developed across the plate load resistor (R-6). As a varying current is drawn by the plate of the 12SQ7, there is a varying voltage drop across the resistor that is applied to the grid of the 50L6 output tube. Condenser C-7 filters out any remaining i.f. signal. Condenser C-3 acts to keep the high voltage from the plate of the 12SQ7 off the grid of the output tube.

In the power output circuit, the signal from the first audio tube is applied to the control grid of the 50L6 power output tube. This grid is given a ground return through resistor R-6. R-6 is not high enough in resistance to give the tube much negative grid bias, so bias for the tube is obtained by placing resistor R-5 in the cathode circuit. Current flowing through the tube causes the cathode to become slightly positive, which is the same thing as making the grid negative by an equal amount.

The second, or screen grid is attached to B+ directly. The beam forming plates in this beam power tube serve much the same function as the suppressor grid in a pentode and are connected to the cathode. The plate of the 50L6 receives its B+ through the primary of the output transformer, T-3, developing its signal in that primary. Condenser C-3, called the tone condenser, softens the tone by removing the higher audio frequencies. It also helps remove background noise.

T-3, the output transformer, transfers the audio signal energy to the very light and low impedance voice coil of the permanent magnet (p.m.) speaker. When the varying current flows through this coil, it reacts with the magnetic field in the loudspeaker, moving the cone of the speaker and producing sound.

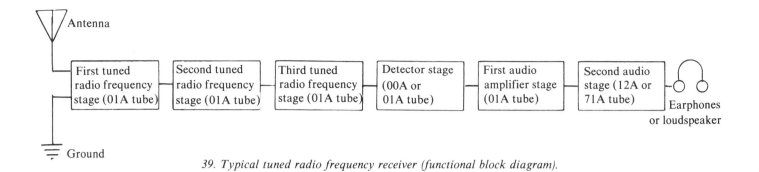

39. *Typical tuned radio frequency receiver (functional block diagram).*

40. *Typical tuned radio frequency receiver (circuit diagram).*

Tuned Radio Frequency Receivers

Figures 39 and 40 show a typical tuned radio frequency receiver from the mid-1920s. This was the design used by many classical era receivers. The circuit is straightforward and simple. It can be powered from batteries or from a power pack. Notice that it uses a considerable number of tubes, since all are low amplification triodes.

You can see from the block diagram that the first three tubes are r.f. amplifiers, the fourth is the detector, and the last two are audio amplifiers.

In the power circuits, the filaments of the tubes are all fed from a 6 volt source, usually an auto-type storage battery. The tubes used have 5 volt filaments. There is a fixed series resistor that drops the voltage to the audio tubes. The detector has a rheostat, which controls its filament voltage, acting like a volume control. The r.f. tube filaments are controlled by another rheostat. This will affect the sensitivity of the receiver, that is, its ability to receive distant stations. Usually the two rheostats are set to give the best tone and volume.

The B voltage must be supplied at three different voltage levels. The three r.f. tubes and the first audio tube require 67½ volts. The output tube needs a higher voltage that depends on the type of tube used. The detector requires only 22½ volts. The 67½ volt line is bypassed to ground through a fixed paper condenser, helping to prevent oscillation.

The antenna circuit usually requires an outside antenna and a good ground. The antenna transformer has a tapped primary to match the impedance of different length antennas. In practice you would try each tap and use the one that works best. The secondary winding of this transformer is tuned by a variable condenser to the frequency desired. There is a small condenser in parallel with the tuning condenser to help match the antenna to the coil.

The tuning condensers in this and other r.f. sections may be fastened together with belts or be on the same shaft so that all are tuned at once. In other sets each may be tuned separately, a difficult job at best.

The three r.f. amplifier stages are identical. In each grid circuit, the secondary of the r.f. transformer, being tuned to resonate with the desired frequency, will reduce other frequencies giving stronger amplification of the desired station. This selection will increase in each stage. There is a small fixed resistor in each grid circuit to aid stability.

A small amount of grid bias is obtained by having the filament go positive from B-, which is also ground. This is done by connecting B- and A- together. The grid will see this as if it were a negative potential on the grid.

The plate of each tube is coupled through the primary of an r.f. transformer to the next stage, receiving its B+ through the primary.

Detection is aided in this triode tube in two ways. First, there is a comparatively large negative grid bias on the tube

57

because of a high resistance grid leak. The grid condenser in the grid circuit keeps the bias on the grid, so that it does not leak off through the transformer. This high bias encourages plate current cutoff on negative swings of the grid.

The other fact encouraging rectification is the low plate voltage (22½ volts) that operates the tube near the bottom of its conducting range, again keeping it from conducting if the grid is very negative.

Thus the signal passes and is amplified only when it is positive enough to overcome the grid bias and the low plate voltage. The fixed resistors that connect the grid leak to the filament and complete the grid circuit also balance the grid in relation to both ends of the filament. The "phone condenser" filters out the r.f. portion of the rectified output, leaving only the audio.

The first audio tube works exactly as the r.f. amplifier tubes do, with one exception. The coupling between stages is done using iron core transformers, which are more efficient than air core transformers at audio frequencies.

Generally, the tube used in the output tube circuit is designed to carry more current and thus to supply the greater power needed to operate the listening device. It differs from the first audio amplifier in a couple of ways. First, it uses C battery bias to set firmly the negative grid bias in order to give the most undistorted output for the tube type chosen. Second, it is coupled directly to the listening device. The plate current of the output tube flows through the earphones or magnetic speaker. Since the current varies with the audio frequency signal, the variations produce sound.

Regenerative Receivers

A simple receiver system, commonly used in early one-tube sets and later as a detector in some TRF receivers, is called the regenerative detector. It is an oscillator tube arrangement that is not quite allowed to oscillate.

Examine figure 41 to see how it works. The antenna picks up a mixture of r.f. signals, causing a small current to flow in the primary of coil L-1 to ground. This current is stepped up in voltage in the secondary, which has more turns of wire. The secondary of L-1 is tuned to resonate at the frequency desired by tuning condenser C-2. This acts to select the desired station. This selected signal is sent to the grid of the triode tube through condenser C-1. The tube then amplifies the signal selected. As electrons flow from filament to plate in the tube, some collect on the grid. They leak off through the high resistance, R-1, but a rather high negative bias remains on the grid.

The tube, in a way similar to the TRF detector, only amplifies the positive part of the signal on the grid, acting as a rectifier. In order to increase amplification and sensitivity, part of the amplified signal on the plate is fed back into the grid by means of tickler winding L-1. It is fed back in such a way as to increase the signal on the grid, forcing the tube to amplify itself.

If too much signal is fed back, the tube becomes an oscillator and all signal is lost. If the right amount is fed back, the tube becomes a very powerful amplifier. The tickler winding is made movable so the coupling can be varied for the right amount of feedback. Once the signal is amplified, it is smoothed by C-3, with the high frequency r.f. being removed. The signal current to the plate flows across the resistance of the headphones, which turn that varying current supplied by the B battery into sound.

Overall volume of the receiver is controlled by the filament rheostat, R-3.

A simpler triode tube type detector can be made by not using the tickler winding. This becomes the simple grid leak detector, which usually needs outside amplification to be effective.

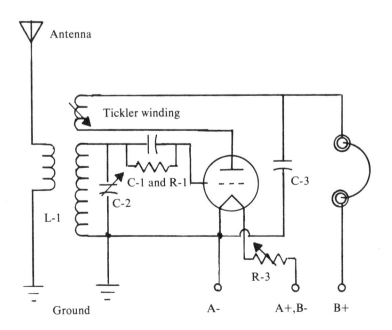

41. Typical one-tube regenerative receiver.

Atwater Kent, model 318, 1934.

Atwater Kent, model 447 chassis (restored), 1935. Cog Hogden, owner.

Crosley, probably model 635, 1935. Photographed at Museum of Wonderful Wireless.

Zenith, model 6V27, 1935, six volt battery, three band. Cog Hogden, owner.

Zenith, chassis number R107260. Photographed at St. Louis Museum of Science and Natural History.

Sentinal, 1937, battery. Photographed at Museum of Wonderful Wireless.

Silvertone, 1937, battery. Photographed at Museum of Wonderful Wireless.

Ferguson, ca. 1936, AC/DC, two band. Photographed at Western Heritage Museum.

Philco, model 37-63, 1937. Photographed at Western Heritage Museum.

Zenith, model 6D311, 1938, AC/DC. Photographed at St. Louis Museum of Science and Natural History.

Truetone RCP, battery, made for Western Auto. Photographed at Museum of Wonderful Wireless.

Zenith, model 5R312, 1938.

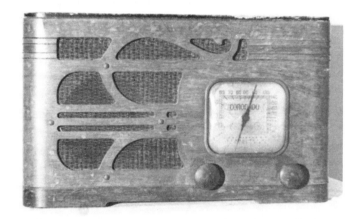

Zenith, model 5S126. Photographed at Western Heritage Museum.

Coronado, model 552, 1939, battery.

Zenith, model 4K331, 1939, battery. Photographed at Museum of Wonderful Wireless.

Crosley, model 527A. Photographed at St. Louis Museum of Science and Natural History.

Zenith, serial number N-154632, three band. Photographed at Western Heritage Museum.

Philco, model 39-70, 1939, battery.

Philco, model 40-95, 1940, battery.

RCA, model 16X13, table radio. Photographed at St. Louis Museum of Science and Natural History.

Philco, model 39-80, 1939, battery, console. Photographed at Western Heritage Museum.

Philco, model 41-95, 1941, battery. Photographed at Western Heritage Museum.

U.S. Navy Multitester, World War II.

RCA, model 55X, 1941, AC/DC. Photographed at Western Heritage Museum.

Philco, model 41-220, 1941, AC/DC, two band. Photographed at Western Heritage Museum.

Musicaire, model 891 CAE, sold by Coast-to-Coast Stores.

Woolroc, model 3-11A, 1946, sold by Phillips Petroleum.

Lincoln, model 5A-110, 1947, AC/DC.

Westinghouse, model H-171, 1946, radio-phonograph.

Philco, model 47-204, 1947. Photographed at Western Heritage Museum.

RCA, velocity microphone ("Junior Velocity"), 1948, used in radio stations and public address systems.

Emerson, model 559, 1948, battery/AC, portable.

Philco, model 49-500, 1949, AC/DC. Photographed at Western Heritage Museum.

Philco, model 51-530, 1951, AC/DC. Photographed at Western Heritage Museum.

Crosley, model 9-105, 1949. Photographed at Museum of Wonderful Wireless.

Dumont, model RA-346, AC/DC, red Chinese-lacquer front. Photographed at Western Heritage Museum.

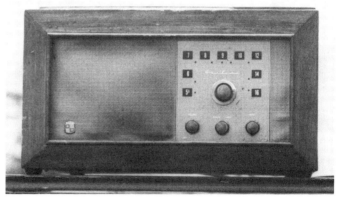

Airline radio-phonograph, model 25GSG-2016A, early 1950s, sold by Montgomery Ward.

67

Zenith, model H500 ("Transoceanic"), postwar, battery/AC.

A, B battery pack for Zenith "Transoceanic."

Emud Rekord, junior model 196, postwar, West Germany. Photographed at Museum of Wonderful Wireless.

Appendix A
Equipment,
Supplies, and Techniques

Test Equipment

These suggestions are listed in the order we consider them important. No beginner would want or could afford all of these, but some are almost essential. When you buy a piece of test equipment, read the accompanying instructions carefully and keep them. Buy books on the use of that equipment.

Multitester. This volt-ohm-milliampmeter is your single most useful electrical tool. Multitesters are available from many sources. An adequate unit costs from $20 to $50.

Your tester should have at least 10,000 ohms per volt sensitivity on the DC voltage scale. It should be capable of measuring resistances of up to 1 megohm accurately. The meter type of tester is fine for your work. The newer digital units cost more and are more accurate, but not that much more helpful.

Radio Shack stores sell a wide variety of multitesters. They also sell a good book on VOM-VTVMs, which will give you a great deal of help in using your tester and doing any electrical testing.

Series light tester. This is not necessary if you plan to buy an isolation transformer. You can build a series light tester by mounting two surface-type porcelain light sockets on a suitably sized board. Use the types that are sold for basement ceilings. Wire in series with a regular lamp cord and plug, as you can see in figures 42 and 43.

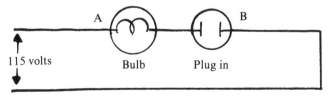

42. Series light tester circuit.

43. Series light tester layout (top view).

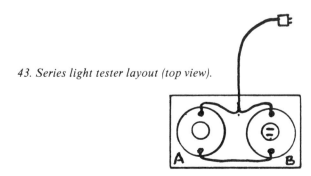

By screwing a plug-in adapter into one socket and a high wattage (200 watts or so) light bulb into the other socket, you have a unit that will protect anything plugged into it. The higher the wattage bulb used, the higher the output voltage will be at the plug-in socket. Remember to tape any open wire connections for safety.

Signal injector. Radio Shack stores sell one for $5.49. This little device produces a broad band electrical signal that can be used to test both r.f. and a.f. amplifier stages. It is not particularly useful in tuning or aligning a set. You don't need one if you plan to buy the more useful r.f. signal generator following.

Isolation transformer. This device protects you from the 115 volt line while it gives you a way to vary widely the output voltage in testing your radio. It will allow you to increase the line voltage fed to an AC set a step at a time, which can help you find power supply problems before they cause damage. It will allow you to run an intermittent radio at a high line voltage to help spot intermittent causes. It will completely protect you from line shock hazard on an AC/DC set.

Isolation transformers are not easy to find but are highly recommended for the serious restorer. They are not inexpensive. We use a VIZ WP-27A unit, which is available from Fordham Radio, 855 Conklin St., Farmingdale, N.Y. 11735.

Tube tester. So far as we know, no one manufactures a tester today that will test the four-, five-, six-, and seven-pin tubes found in older sets. Used tube testers that will do this can be found at older radio repair shops or from other radio amateurs. Check the ads in newsletters that serve antique radio collectors. They cost anywhere from $10 to $100. We bought ours for $15.

R.F. signal generator. A signal generator, which will produce modulated signals of any frequency you need, is almost essential for any aligning of radios, and is very helpful in troubleshooting. Try to find a unit that will produce signals from 100 kHz. to at least 20 MHz. These are available from any radio service supply source, such as Fordham Radio (see above).

Signal generators can be built from a kit. Heathkit sells a battery operated kit for about $50. Eico has several models. We use an Eico Model 324 generator, which costs $90 as a kit or $127 ready-built.

Test loudspeaker. You can make one from an old permanent magnet speaker in a cabinet and an output transformer from an old radio, and be able to use the speaker without the output transformer or with it. If you are going to couple this to an output tube directly, as in a classical era set, you will need the transformer. The speaker can be used directly to replace a p.m. or a dynamic speaker. If you use it to test a field coil speaker, leave the field coil on the original speaker connected to the set.

Oscilloscope. This TV-like instrument allows you to see the nature of the waveform of any electrical signal in a set. It is useful for signal tracing, finding distortion, spotting high frequency oscillations, and so on, but not essential. It is expensive. If you buy one, get a "triggered sweep" type. Heathkit has a line of 'scopes starting at $250 in kit form. A unit for the serious hobbyist will cost from $250 to $500. Professional electronics service personnel use 'scopes a great deal.

Shop Tools

Most of the following are available at Wards, Sears, or Radio Shack.
- Soldering iron (30 watts or more).
- Long-nose pliers. (Buy the best you can. We have used one pair for over thirty years, and it is still good.)
- Diagonal wire cutter. (Again, buy a good one.)
- Small screwdrivers, phillips and regular.
- Nut driver set.
- Utility knife.
- Set of plastic alignment tools.
- Soldering aids. (These look like dentist tools and are useful for prying, twisting, and poking things into place. Buy both the split-end and bent-end types.)
- Insulated test wires with clips at both ends. (Buy half a dozen.)

Shop Supplies

- Solder. (60 percent tin—40 percent lead rosin core.)
- Desoldering braid. (This is useful for cleaning solder from a connection you wish to take apart.)
- TV tuner-cleaner spray.
- Black electrical tape.
- Pack of colored tapes. (These are useful for marking wires and connections.)
- WD-40 lubricant spray.
- Silicon dry lubricant spray.
- Dry powdered rosin. (Obtain from a music store.)

Useful Substitute Testing or Replacement Parts

- 20 mfd. 450 volt electrolytic capacitor.
- .1 mfd. 600 volt capacitor.
- .01 mfd. 600 volt capacitor.
- 100 ohm 10 watt resistor.
- 250,000 ohm volume control.
- 470,000 ohm ½ watt carbon resistor.
- 100,000 ohm ½ watt carbon resistor.
- 10,000 ohm ½ watt carbon resistor.
- 2,200 ohm ½ watt carbon resistor.
- 470 ohm ½ watt carbon resistor.

Shop Tips

Removing parts (desoldering connections). Heat the joint you wish to disconnect carefully with a soldering iron. As the solder starts to melt, use desoldering braid to soak up the melted solder. After it cools, cut off soaked end of braid. Bare copper braid must always touch the joint. When you have removed as much solder as you can in this way, use the soldering tool with the double end to work the wire loose. You may be able to cut away parts of the wire to get it loose. Remove bits that you cut from the chassis.

Sometimes the job can be made easier by cutting away the part to be removed, leaving about 1/8" at the joint. It may be easier to work the wire end out. Other times, if you are disposing of the part, it may be as easy to cut it away leaving about ½" of wire. This can then be twisted around the wire from the new part, and the wires soldered.

Caution: Do not splash solder around the chassis or tube socket. Solder splashes can cause short circuits.

Soldering. The surfaces to be soldered must be clean. Steel wool can be used AWAY from the chassis to clean parts.

Caution: Do not use steel wool near or in the chassis. The bits of steel that come from the pad can cause serious problems by short circuiting components or by being picked up by the loudspeaker magnet.

When making a connection to a terminal or another wire, make a mechanical bond by hooking in the wire. Touch the joint with the iron, heating it for a few seconds. Touch solder to the point where the iron touches the joint. Melt on just enough solder to cover the joint. Remove iron and cool the joint with pliers.

Caution: Do not heat the joint longer than necessary to flow on the solder smoothly. Excessive and prolonged heat will sometimes damage condensers and resistors. If not enough heat is used, the joint will have insufficient solder flow. This joint will develop a high resistance later and give trouble. You want solder to flow over the entire joint with the wire.

Burns. You probably will get small burns from your soldering iron or solder splashes. If you do, immediately run cold water over it, even if it doesn't hurt. Every time it starts to hurt, cool it again with water. Cover it only if it has blistered or if the skin is broken.

Electrical shock danger. This is important! Do not work on electrical equipment in an environment where you are grounded, that is, where any part of your body or work surface can contact ground.

If you must work in a basement, try to work on an insulated surface. A sheet of tempered masonite on the floor under your bench is a good idea. Do not use a metal stool in a basement.

High voltages are dangerous if they can flow through any major part of your body. Before you touch anything inside a chassis that has power applied to it, know what you are doing. Try not to use both hands in a chassis that is under power. Do not hold the chassis with one hand while poking with the other.

If you are soldering or removing parts or even cleaning out debris, do so with the radio unplugged!

Whenever you are in doubt about what voltages exist and where, let your voltmeter precede you.

Philco, model F675-124, AC/DC/battery, portable. Photographed at Western Heritage Museum.

Westinghouse, model H-127, AC/DC, portable. Photographed at Western Heritage Museum.

Adventures of Slim and Spud—Caught!

Appendix B Information on Common Tubes

Basic information on some common tubes is necessary when testing filaments or identifying pins on a tube socket for making voltage tests. The diagrams show a bottom view. For more information on tube operation, see chapter 2.

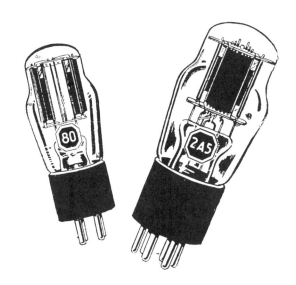

44. Old tubes.

Number	Base Diagram	Filament Voltage	Maximum Plate Voltage	Type
'01A	4A	5 v.	135 v.	Triode
2A5	6A	2.5 v.	375 v.	Power pentode
5Y3	8K	5 v.	-	Rectifier (double diode)
6A7	7A	6.3 v.	300 v.	Pentagrid converter
6A8	8A	6.3 v.	300 v.	Pentagrid converter
6C6	6B	6.3 v.	300 v.	Pentode
6C7	7B	6.3 v.	250 v.	Dual diode, triode
6D6	6B	6.3 v.	300 v.	R.F. pentode

6F6	8J	6.3 v.	375 v.	Power pentode
6F7	7C	6.3 v.	250 v.	Triode, pentode
6K8	8B	6.3 v.	300 v.	Triode, hexode converter
6Q7	8H	6.3 v.	300 v.	Dual diode, triode
6SA7	8C	6.3 v.	300 v.	Pentagrid converter
6SK7	8D	6.3 v.	300 v.	R.F. pentode
6SQ7	8E	6.3 v.	300 v.	Dual diode, triode
'12A	4A	5 v.	180 v.	Triode
12SA7	8C	12.6 v.	300 v.	Pentagrid converter
12SK7	8D	12.6 v.	300 v.	R.F. pentode
12SQ7	8E	12.6 v.	300 v.	Dual diode, triode
24A	5B	2.5 v.	250 v.	R.F. pentode
25L6	8G	25 v.	200 v.	Beam power amplifier
25Z5	6C	25 v.	-	Rectifier (double diode)
26	4A	1.5 v.	180 v.	Triode
27	5C	2.5 v.	275 v.	Triode
35L6	8G	35 v.	200 v.	Beam power amplifier
35Z5	8F	35 v.	-	Rectifier (single diode)
36	5B	6.3 v.	250 v.	R.F. tetrode
39/44	5D	6.3 v.	250 v.	R.F. pentode
41	6A	6.3 v.	315 v.	Power pentode
42	6A	6.3 v.	375 v.	Power pentode
43	6A	25 v.	160 v.	Power pentode
45	4A	2.5 v.	275 v.	Power triode
47	5A	2.5 v.	250 v.	Power pentode
50L6	8G	50 v.	200 v.	Beam power amplifier
56	5C	2.5 v.	250 v.	Triode
58	6B	2.5 v.	300 v.	R.F. pentode

'71A	4A	5 v.	180 v.	Power triode
75	6D	6.3 v.	250 v.	Dual diode, triode
76	5C	6.3 v.	250 v.	Triode
80	4B	5 v.	-	Rectifier (double diode)

Tube pins are marked on the diagrams with the following letter identifications:
F=Filament. G=Grid. H=heater. P= Plate. HL=Heater tap for panel lamp. K=Cathode.

Tube identifiers. Later tubes with octal bases used an identifying system consisting of a number, one or more letters, and a number. Sometimes in reading circuit diagrams, you will find that one or more letters follow the last number, for example, 6F6, 6F6G, 6F6GT. All three are power output tubes of the pentode type. The 6F6 is a metal shell tube, the 6F6G is a glass tube with a large shell, and the 6F6GT is a glass tube with a smaller tubular shell. These would usually be interchangeable. Sometimes, in r.f. amplification or mixer use, the metal tube with its built-in shielding will work where a glass one will not. The glass tube would be all right if it had an outside metal shield attached.

Old tube identifiers. Tubes like '01A, '12A, and '71A will usually be identified on the tube and in diagrams with a 1, 2, or 3 leading number, for example, 101A, 201A, and 301A. The first number refers to the manufacturer and has nothing to do with the tubes' characteristics. The 1, 2, and 3 tubes are interchangeable. In some literature, a tube will be identified as '01A or simply a 01A.

Purchasing replacement tubes. Before buying a replacement tube, check prices of two or more sources, if possible. We have found tubes can cost four times as much from one source to another. It pays to shop around.

Tube cartons, including two of the last vacuum tubes designed (center middle, a compactron; center bottom, a nuvistor).

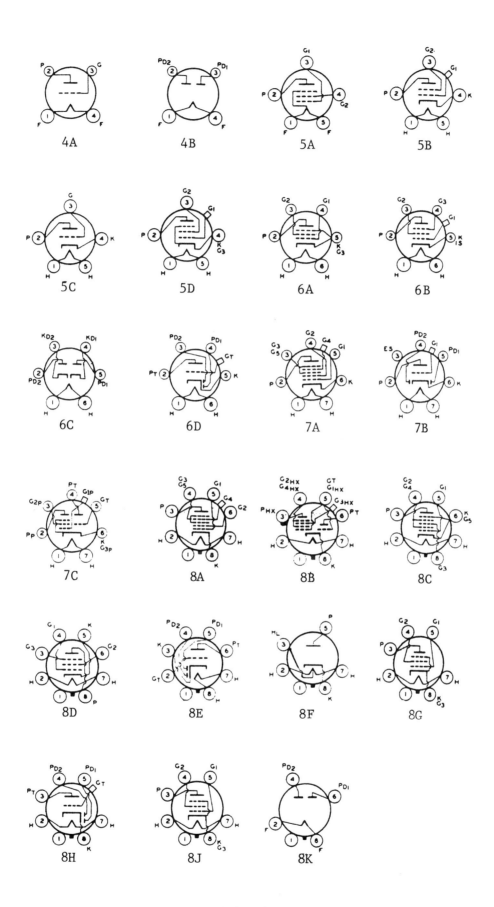

45. Tube base diagrams.

Appendix C Sources of Parts and Diagrams

This is a very limited listing of parts and supplies sources. The best way to keep up on what is available in this ever-changing hobby is to subscribe to one or more of the hobby newsletters listed in Appendix D.

Antenna Systems

The Antique Apparatus Co. 11650 Riverside Drive, North Hollywood, CA 91602

Radio Shack. (retail stores)

Battery Eliminators

The Sound Box. Box 313, Ettrick, WI 54627

Circuit Diagrams

Puett Electronics. P.O. Box 28572, Dallas, TX 75228

Olde Tyme Radio. 2445 Lyttonsville Rd., Silver Spring, MD 20910

ARS Electronics. 646 Kenilworth Terrace, Kenilworth, IL 60043. (Source for the highly useful Superior service manuals)

Finishing Supplies and Veneers

The Woodworkers' Store. 21801 Industrial Boulevard, Rogers, MN 55374

Craftsman Wood Service Co. 1735 W. Cortland Ct., Addison, IL 60101

Knobs and Dials

Keith Parry. 17557 Horace St., Granada Hills, CA 91344

S.R. Danielson. 5633 Emerson Ave. S., Minneapolis, MN 55419

Loudspeaker Repairs

White's Reconing Service. 2825 Jefferson Ave., Davenport, IA 52803

Dixie Speaker Repair. 549 Shades Crest Rd., Birmingham, AL 35226

Treeman-Tuell Speaker Repair Service. 7720 Ferguson Rd., Dallas, TX 75228

Miscellaneous Parts and Supplies

Roaring 20's. F.A. Paul. 1545 Raymond, Glendale, CA 91201

Olde Tyme Radio. 2445 Lyttonsville Rd., Silver Spring, MD 20910

Puett Electronics. P.O. Box 28572, Dallas, TX 75228

Tubes

ARS Electronics. 646 Kenilworth Terrace, Kenilworth, IL 60043

Fair Radio Sales Co., Inc. P.O. Box 1105, Lima, OH

Olde Tyme Radio. 2445 Lyttonsville Rd., Silver Spring, MD 20910

Puett Electronics. P.O. Box 28572, Dallas, TX 75228

Richardson Electronics Ltd. 3030 North River Road, Franklin Park, IL 60131

Sam Faust. Changewater, NJ 07831

Unity Electronics. Elizabeth Industrial Park, 107 Trumbull St., Elizabeth, NJ 07206

Transformer Rewinding

Richard Ray. 423 Orchard, Canon City, CO 81212

Appendix D Sources of Information

Books

Alth, Max. *Collecting Old Radios and Crystal Sets.* Des Moines, Iowa: Wallace-Homestead Books, 1977.

Beitman, Morris. *Most Often Needed 1926-1938 Radio Diagrams.* North Highlands, Calif.: Vintage Radio, n.d.

Cannon, William A. *How to Cast Small Metal & Rubber Parts.* Blue Ridge Summit, Pa.: Tab Books, 1979.

Ghirardi, Alfred A. *Modern Radio Servicing.* New York: Radio & Technical Publishing Co., 1935. Out of print; excellent course in servicing radios manufactured in the 1930s.

Radio Trouble-Shooters Handbook. New York: Radio & Technical Publishing Co., 1938. Out of print; lists things most likely to go wrong on old radios by make and model, a great help in locating problems.

Hallmark, Clayton L. *How to Repair Old-time Radios.* Blue Ridge Summit, Pa.: Tab Books, 1979. Good advanced restoration guide.

McMahon, Morgan E. *A Flick of the Switch: 1930-1950.* North Highlands, Calif.: Vintage Radio, 1975.

Radio Collector's Guide: 1921-1932. Rev. ed. North Highlands, Calif.: Vintage Radio, 1981. Specifications for most radios of the era, including cabinet styles, circuits, stages, and even automobile radios.

Paul, Floyd A. *The Horn Speaker Notebook.* Rev. B. Glendale, Calif.: Floyd A. Paul, 1981. Available from F.A. Paul, 1545 Raymond, Glendale, CA 91201.

Puett, J.W.F. *The Antique Radio Restoration Handbook.* Dallas, Tex.: Puett Electronics, 1981-date, issued irregularly. From Puett Electronics, P.O. Box 28592, Dallas, TX 75228. Two volumes available. Each about twenty pages, and contains much useful information.

The Encyclopedia of Antique Radio. Dallas, Tex.: Puett Electronics, 1979-date, issued irregularly. Available from Puett Electronics at the above address.

Radio Corporation of America. *Radio Enters the Home.* 1922. Reprint. Vestal, N.Y.: Vestal Press, n.d. Lots of information, besides being interesting to read.

Receiving Tube Guide. Kenilworth, Ill.: ARS Electronics, 1981. Available from ARS Electronics, 646 Kenilworth Terr., Kenilworth, IL 60043.

Sams, Howard W., Editorial Staff. *Basic Electricity and an Introduction to Electronics.* Indianapolis, Ind.: Howard W. Sams, 1973.

Swedberg, Robert W., and Swedberg, Harriett. *Off Your Rocker: Guide to Furniture Refinishing.* Des Moines, Iowa: Wallace-Homestead Book Co., 1976.

Used books are available from Radiographics Books, P.O. Box 18492, Cleveland Heights, Ohio 44118.

Magazines

Specialty magazines contain much useful information that isn't readily available elsewhere. Prices change rapidly, so check with the publisher before sending your money.

Antique Radio Topics & The Classic Radio Newsletter. P.O. Box 28572, Dallas, TX 75228. $15.00/year. 6 issues. Particularly useful for collectors of E.H. Scott and McMurdo Silver radios.

Electronics Trader. P.O. Box 73, Folly Beach, SC 29439. $7.50/year. 24 issues. Shopper for anything from early tubes to modern test gear.

The Horn Speaker. 9820 Silver Meadow Dr., Dallas, TX 75217. $7.00/year. Monthly, except July and August.

Old Timer's Bulletin. Main St., Holcomb, N.Y. 14469. $6.50/year (includes membership in the Antiques Wireless Association). Quarterly.

Radio Age. 636 Cambridge Rd., Augusta, GA 30909. $8.75/year. Monthly, except July and August.

Clubs

Old radio clubs are springing up all over the country. To find one in your region contact the Antique Wireless Association (Main St., Holcomb, NY 14469) or the Canadian Vintage Wireless Association (c/o J. Knott, 69 Rossburn, Drive, Etobicoke, Ontario M9C 2P9, Canada). Public libraries often have lists of local clubs and may have a radio club listed.

Museums

Museums featuring old radios are still few and far between. We list several specialty museums below, as well as general museums that have sizable radio collections. However, exhibits are changed, so check first with the museum to avoid driving out of your way only to find that the radios are in storage. Several museums are open "by appointment only." These are usually private collections, operated by men who have been interested in radio from its early days and who love to talk about radio. They are proud of their collections and enjoy showing them off, so don't be reluctant to write them. They'll enjoy your visit.

Alabama

J. Herbert Orr Museum of Sound. 1203 Crawford Rd., Opelika, AL 36801. Open: By appointment only. Contact: J. Herbert Orr at this address or telephone (205) 749-8261. Very large collection of old radios and phonographs.

Arkansas

The Castle. Route 2, Box 375, Eureka Springs, AR 72632. Open: Daily, 15 April-31 November (9:00 A.M.-5:00 P.M.). A general museum, specializing in tools, implements, and devices used in the area in the early 1900s. Has over fifty radios.

California

Foothill Electronics Museum. Foothill College, 12345 El Monte Rd., Los Altos Hills, CA 94022. Open: Thursday and Friday (9:00 A.M.-4:30 P.M.); Sunday (1:00-4:00 P.M.). A large collection of over 400 radios, ranging from crystal to modern.

Illinois

Old Radio Museum. Pequod Pizza Restaurant, 8520 N. Fernald St., Morton Grove, IL 60053. Open: Tuesday-Thursday (11:00 A.M.-1:00 P.M.; 4:00-10:00 P.M.); Friday (11:00 A.M.-1:00 P.M.; 4:00-12 P.M.); Saturday (4:00-12 P.M.); Sunday (4:00-10:00 P.M.). About 250 radios, specializing in pre-1923 ham gear and spark transmitters.

Indiana

Auburn-Cord-Duesenberg Museum. 1600 S. Wayne St., P.O. Box 148, Auburn, IN 46706. Open: Daily (9:00 A.M.-7:00 P.M.). About 125 radios.

Minnesota

Museum of Wonderful Wireless. 2632 Nicollet Ave., Minneapolis, MN 55408. Open: By appointment only. Contact Joe Pavek at this address or telephone (612) 872-0885. Three rooms of radios. Collection is strongest in pre-1930 radios and those of Minnesota manufacture. Good source for data about old sets.

Missouri

Museum of Science and Natural History. Oak Knoll Park, St. Louis, MO 63105. Open: Winter, Tuesday-Saturday (9:00 A.M.-5:00 P.M.); Sunday (1:00-5:00 P.M.). Summer, Daily (9:00 A.M.-5:00 P.M.). About 100 radios.

Nebraska

Western Heritage Museum. 801 S. 10th St., Omaha, NB 68108. Open: Tuesday-Friday (10:00 A.M.-5:00 P.M.); Saturday and Sunday (1:00-5:00 P.M.). Approximately 100 radios, including a collection of DeForest radios.

New Jersey

U.S. Army Communications-Electronics Museum. Myer Hall, Ave. of Memories, Fort Monmouth, NJ 07703. Open: Monday-Friday (8:00 A.M.-4:00 P.M.). Includes some commercial radios, but primarily interested in military communication, including military radio.

The W2ZI Historical Wireless Museum. 19 Blackwood Dr., Trenton, NJ 08628. Open: By appointment only. Contact Ed Raser at this address or telephone (609) 882-6645. Over 400 pieces of apparatus on display, with specialties in amateur equipment and early commercial sets.

South Carolina

The WCSC Broadcast Museum. 80 Alexander St., Charleston, SC 29401. Open: Closed for renovation; open in 1983. Contact WSCS-TV at telephone (803) 723-8371 for hours. Four rooms of radios.

Texas

Harrison County Historical Museum. Old Courthouse, Peter Whetstone Sq., Marshall, TX 75670. Open: Sunday-Friday (1:30-5:00 P.M.). Closed holidays and the weeks preceding and including Christmas. Small collection of about twenty-five radios manufactured before 1935.

Texas Broadcast Museum. 1701 N. Market St., Dallas, TX 75202. Open: Tuesday-Friday (10:00 A.M.-6:00 P.M.); Saturday and Sunday (11:00 A.M.-7:00 P.M.). A "hands-on" museum, with things to do, old programs to hear, and exhibits to view. 125 radios, no specialty.

Canada

National Museum of Science and Technology. 1867 St. Laurent Blvd., Ottawa, Ontario K1G 1A3, Canada. Open: By appointment only for radio collection. Contact E.A. Decoste or T. Paull at this address or telephone (613) 998-9520. Between 150 and 200 radios, either made or designed in Canada.

Appendix E   Price Guide

Price guides are simply that—guides to prices. Use ours as such, and not as the final word on what a radio is worth, particularly since the market value of radios in general is not yet established. Pricing radios is difficult because there are two groups of collectors with completely dissimilar tastes. One group is interested in technical aspects of radio and early sets. The other group collects interesting cabinets first and, secondarily, sets. Whereas one collector will pay a lot for a cathedral radio because of its looks, another collector will not, because technically it isn't very interesting.

Assume the following radios are table models unless otherwise stated. The same model number may identify both a console and a table model. If the listing does not mention console (and that includes low-boys and high-boys), expect that the console will cost more than the price listed. To confuse things even more, some companies made several different cabinets varying greatly in construction and price for the same radio and used the same model number for all of them.

Dates are approximate, but probably accurate to within one year. On early radios, dates were checked where possible with McMahon's *Radio Collector's Guide*. On later radios, dates were obtained from service manuals, advertisements, and radio literature. Some radios were produced over several years with no change of model numbers; the dates listed here are for the earliest models.

Prices here reflect a reasonable plus-or-minus factor of 20 percent. That is, if a radio is listed at $100, a price between $80 and $120 is reasonable. The prices of battery sets do not include separate speakers. Tubes are included. If tubes are missing in an early radio, plan to spend $40-50 on these and adjust your price for the radio accordingly.

Prices also assume that a radio is in good to very good condition. Plan to spend more for a radio in excellent condition. Plan to spend a lot more if the radio is a classic set in excellent condition.

Specialties are subject to their own pricing because they are collecting fields in their own right. Thus, unusual radios (Mickey Mouse, New York World's Fair, etc.), mirror radios, and radios made by certain companies (E.H. Scott, Silver Marshall) are not included here.

This guide is designed to be used with the radios you're most likely to find outside of restoration radio dealers and fancy antique shops. That explains the large number of listings for Crosley, Philco, RCA, and Zenith radios and the relatively few listings for some of the more classic sets.

Thumbnail prices to be used with caution, but helpful in the absence of more specific information, are: cathedrals ($100-125, up); tombstones ($60-80); console radio-phonographs from late 1940s ($25); small plastic table radios ($1-15).

Radio	Date	Model	Battery	A/C	Price
A.C.Dayton	1923	(crystal set)			$100
	1924	Super Polydyne 6	x		125
	1925	XL-5	x		85
	1926	XL-25	x		60
	1929	AC-9970 "Navigator" (console)		x	115
	1929	AC-98		x	70
Adams-Morgan	1921	Paragon RA-10	x		200
Adler	1924	201-A	x		75
Admiral	1936	AM786 (console)		x	30
	1938	123-5E		x	8
	1939	162-5L		x	10
	1939	361-5Q		x	7
	1940	34-F5 (portable)	x	x	under 5
	1951	5J21		x	8
Aerodyne	1927	Special	x		75
Air King	1933	(with clock)		x	45
	1947	A-403 "Court Jester"		x	15
	1947	4604 (AM/SW)		x	11
	1948	A-4000		x	6
Air-Way	1924	41	x		80
Aircastle	1948	179 (portable)	x		under 5
Airline	1926	"Roamer" (portable)	x		120
	1938	62-606		x	10
	1948	64BR-1808A		x	13
	1948	74BR-1053A		x	under 5
	1948	74BR-1057A		x	5
	1948	74KR-1210A	x	x	5
	1949	84BR-1065A (portable)	x	x	7
	1949	84HA-2725A (AM/FM/phono; console)		x	20
	1949	94BR-1535A (AM/FM)		x	15
	1951	056AA-992A (radio/three-speed phono)		x	11
	1951	94HA-1528C		x	9
Airway	1924	41	x		70
Alden	1949	1903		x	5
Algene	1948	AR-406 (portable)	x		under 5
Algonquin	1927	RF-5	x		100
American Bosch	1925	16 "Amborola"	x		235
	1931	5A		x	30
	1933	350 (two band)		x	20
	1933	360T (multiband)		x	60
	1934	402		x	35
	1935	430T (three band)		x	45
	1935	505		x	40
	1936	660T (multiband)		x	15
Amrad	1925	T5	x		55
	1929	81 "Serenata" (console)		x	180
Amsco	1923	"Melco Supreme"	x		125
Andrews	1925	Deresnadyne	x		70

Radio	Date	Model	Battery	A/C	Price
Apex	1925	Super 5	x		$70
	1948	25		x	5
Arborphone	1926	(no model number)	x		80
	1927	27	x		90
Argus	1926	Standard	x		90
Arvin	1938	58		x	7
	1938	78 (two band)		x	8
	1948	152T		x	5
	1948	182TFM (AM/FM)		x	9
	1948	RE-265		x	9
	1949	341T		x	7
	1950	440T		x	5
Atwater Kent	1923	Radiodyne	x		600
	1923	10	x		250
	1924	20	x		140
	1925	20-C	x		100
	1926	30	x		60
	1926	30 (console;with battery eliminator)	x		100
	1926	32	x		70
	1926	35	x		70
	1927	33	x		80
	1927	36 (with power supply)	x		75
	1927	37	x		85
	1928	40	x		55
	1928	42	x		55
	1928	44	x		65
	1928	48	x		60
	1928	52		x	55
	1928	52 (console)		x	110
	1929	45		x	85
	1929	46		x	85
	1929	55		x	90
	1929	55 (console)		x	145
	1929	60		x	180
	1931	84		x	125
	1932	612 (console)		x	125
	1933	155		x	30
	1933	217 (AM/SW)		x	40
	1933	310 (two band; console)		x	140
	1933	558	x		50
	1934	206 (three band)		x	70
	1934	318		x	75
	1934	318 (console)		x	110
	1934	551W "Tune-o-matic"		x	125
	1935	337 (multiband)		x	65
Audiola	1927	6C (console)	x		70
Beaver	1925	"Baby Grand" (crystal set)			100
Belmont	1938	408	x		8
	1946	6D111		x	12
	1947	6D120		x	12
	1948	4B115		x	8
	1949	A-7DF21 (AM/FM)		x	7

Radio	Date	Model	Battery	A/C	Price
Bendix	1948	613 (radio/phono)		x	$20
	1948	847B (AM/FM/phono; console)		x	30
	1948	416A		x	7
	1949	65P4		x	under 5
	1949	111		x	5
	1949	526E		x	10
Blue Seal	1925	"Cyncodyne"	x		375
Brandeis	1925	"Brandola"	x		75
Bremer Tulley	1926	8 "Counterphase"	x		95
Browning Drake	1927	6-A	x		90
Brunswick	1930	15 (console)		x	90
Buckingham	1926	"Junior"	x		55
Capitol	1949	UN-72 (AM/SW)		x	10
Cardwell	1922	125A	x		85
Case	1926	60A	x		75
Chancellor	1948	35P (portable)	x	x	10
Clapp Eastham	1923	R4	x		50
Clarion	1930	60AC "Junior"		x	125
	1933	470		x	125
Commonwealth	1935	260 (five band)		x	40
Coronado	1939	552	x		12
	1947	43-8160		x	under 5
	1947	43-8437		x	7
	1947	43-8576 (AM/SW)		x	12
	1947	43-7602 (AM/SW/phono; console)		x	25
	1948	43-8240; 43-8241		x	under 5
	1948	43-6301		x	5
	1948	43-6321	x		10
	1948	43-8305		x	under 5
	1948	43-9201 (radio/phono)		x	10
	1951	05RA33		x	7
	1951	43-8330		x	12
Crosley	1922	VI	x		250
	1922	X	x		200
	1923	3B "Ace"	x		55
	1924	50	x		90
	1924	51	x		90
	1924	52	x		90
	1925	"Pup"	x		300
	1926	4-29	x		75
	1926	5-38	x		175
	1926	5-50	x		115
	1927	601 "Bandbox"	x		60
	1928	608 "Gembox"		x	95
	1928	704 "Jewelbox"		x	85
	1928	706 "Showbox"		x	90
	1930	53E "Mate"		x	90
	1932	45		x	105
	1932	"Litlfella"		x	75
	1932	167		x	125
	1934	61(AM/SW)		x	50
	1934	169 (two band)		x	115
	1935	1316 (three band; console)		x	40

Radio	Date	Model	Battery	A/C	Price
	1937	C-516		x	$20
	1938	1217-M (three band; console)		x	30
	1947	66TC-S		x	5
	1947	56TN-L (AM/SW)		x	6
	1947	56FC (AM/SW)	x		under 5
	1948	58TK		x	under 5
	1948	9-101		x	under 5
	1948	56TY		x	5
	1948	56TP-L (AM/SW/phono)		x	15
	1948	9-117	x		under 5
	1948	56TD		x	under 5
	1949	9-214M (AM/FM/phono; console)		x	30
	1949	66XTA (two band)		x	10
	1949	10-145M (radio/phono)		x	13
	1949	9-105		x	9
	1949	10D		x	under 5
DeForest	1920	T-200-P-300	x		160
	1922	DT600 "Everyman" (crystal set)			200
	1922	D6	x		275
	1922	D7	x		275
	1923	D10	x		325
	1924	D12 (with loop antenna)	x		275
	1925	F-5AW	x		225
	1925	F-5M	x		225
	1925	W6	x		250
Delco	1937	R-3208 (four band)	x		10
	1947	R-1408; R1409 (portable)	x	x	under 5
	1947	R-1227; R-1228; R-1229; R-1230; R-1231		x	under 5
	1948	R-1232		x	10
	1948	R-1238		x	6
Detrola	1947	7270 (radio/phono)		x	10
DeWald	1948	B504 (portable)	x	x	5
Dictograph	1937	91134 (pillow speaker)		x	25
ECA	1958	204	x	x	under 5
Echophone	1925	4	x		75
	1932	S-5		x	175
Eckstein	1948	T-5		x	6
Emerson	1933	109		x	25
	1933	250		x	40
	1933	415		x	25
	1934	36		x	30
	1934	71 (four band)		x	50
	1935	38 (two band)		x	30
	1935	108		x	35
	1935	L150 (two band; chairside)		x	75
	1937	A-148		x	25
	1938	AT-172		x	35
	1938	AZ-196(two band)		x	25
	1939	AX-238		x	15
	1946	508		x	10
	1948	536 (portable)	x	x	under 5
	1948	540		x	10

Radio	Date	Model	Battery	A/C	Price
	1948	546 (radio/phono)		x	$12
	1948	547-A		x	under 5
	1948	553-A		x	under 5
	1948	558		x	under 5
	1948	559 (portable)	x	x	10
	1948	561		x	5
	1948	605 (AM/FM; console)		x	15
	1949	581		x	7
	1949	597 (three band)		x	9
	1949	602 (FM only)		x	5
	1949	616		x	11
Edmund Rekord*	50s	196 (multiband)		x	20
Erla	1929	30 (console)		x	90
Eveready	1927	1		x	175
FADA	1925	192A "Neutrolette"	x		100
	1925	160A	x		85
	1927	Special	x		70
Fairbanks Morse	1934	5106		x	125
Farnsworth	1948	GK-699 (AM/SW/Phono;console)		x	35
Federal	1923	DX58	x		200
	1924	61	x		200
	1925	141	x		100
	1925	200	x		175
	1928	H		x	70
	1948	1040-TB		x	under 5
J.B. Ferguson	1925	"TRF"	x		80
Ferrar	1948	C81B (AM/SW; console)		x	25
	1948	T61B (AM/SW)		x	8
Firestone	1948	4-A-1		x	under 5
	1948	4-A-3		x	under 5
	1949	4-A-10		x	5
	1949	4-A-39 (seven band)		x	25
	1949	4-A-37; 4-A-42 (AM/SW/phono; console)		x	40
Freed Eisemann	1924	NR-12	x		125
	1925	FE-15	x		175
	1926	50	x		110
	1927	130	x		65
	1929	NR-55	x		75
	1934	366 (four band)		x	35
	1934	482 (four band)		x	125
	1937	30-D		x	20
Freshman	1924	"Masterpiece"	x		110
	1925	"Masterpiece"	x		125
	1927	G7 "Equaphase"	x		65
Garod	1947	5A1 "Ensign"		x	under 5
	1947	5AP1-Y "Companion" (radio/ phono)		x	9
	1947	5D-3	x	x	under 5
	1948	4A-1		x	7
	1948	5A2-Y		x	under 5

*This is an example of the European radios available in the 1950s. Their price depends on how you like their styling, which is different from American styling. Their electronics are fine.

Radio	Date	Model	Battery	AC/DC	Price
General	1947	4B5		x	under 5
	1947	23A6 (portable)	x	x	under 5
	1947	24B6		x	8
	1947	25B5 (portable)	x	x	under 5
	1948	26B5		x	under 5
	1949	27C5L		x	12
General Electric	1931	S-22		x	75
	1932	J-72		x	125
	1933	K-36		x	125
	1933	K-50		x	45
	1933	K-52 (two band)		x	70
	1933	K-60		x	100
	1933	K-63 (two band)		x	60
	1933	K-80		x	85
	1935	A-63 (two band)		x	50
	1935	A-70 (three band)		x	35
	1935	A-82 (four band)		x	50
	1935	A-125 (three band; console)		x	45
	1937	E-51 (two band)		x	25
	1938	6D-52		x	20
	1938	F-74 (two band)		x	25
	1939	H-116 (three band radio/phono; console)		x	85
	1940	54 (three band)		x	20
	1940	J-809 (radio/phono; console)		x	35
	1941	L-740 (three band)		x	30
	1947	180	x		9
	1947	254	x	x	under 5
	1948	41;42;43 (radio/phono; console)		x	20
	1948	44 (radio/phono; console)		x	25
	1948	45 (radio/phono; console)		x	15
	1948	107W		x	5
	1948	260 (portable)	x		35
	1948	304 (radio/phono)		x	12
	1948	376 (AM/FM; console)		x	25
	1948	YRB 83-1		x	6
	1949	123		x	5
	1949	203		x	12
	1949	357 (AM/FM)		x	10
	1949	X-415 (AM/old FM/new FM/SW)		x	30
	1951	605		x	5
Gloritone	1931	5TRF		x	125
Grebe	1921	CR5	x		200
	1921	CR6	x		400
	1921	CR9	x		300
	1923	CR12	x		175
	1925	MU-1 "Synchophase"	x		150
David Grimes	1925	5B "Baby Grand Duplex"	x		160
	1925	4DL "Inverse Duplex Reflex"	x		175
Grunow	1934	1101 (console; remote control)		x	35
	1937	1291 (three band)		x	35
Hallicrafters	1948	S-53 (multiband)		x	40
Hammarland Roberts	1925	(no model name)	x		165

Radio	Date	Model	Battery	A/C	Price
Howard	1934	"Explorer" (four band; console)		x	$100
	1934	AA25	x	x	25
	1937	B-5 (two band; also part of a Sheaffer's clock-radio-pen set)		x	20
	1947	906		x	5
	1947	472C (AM/FM/phono; chairside)		x	45
	1948	474		x	6
	1948	909-M (AM/SW/phono; console)		x	35
Jackson Bell	1930	62		x	100
Jewel	1948	300		x	11
Kadette	1935	"Jewel"		x	40
	1938	649 (two band; chairside)		x	50
Kennedy	1921	220	x		300
	1923	311 (portable)	x		225
	1931	42		x	75
	1932	53		x	30
Kolster	1925	8B	x		300
	1926	6D	x		75
	1926	6H	x		75
	1929	K45 (console; remote control)		x	125
Lamco	1948	3000 (portable)	x	x	7
Legion	1932	5B		x	60
	1932	6A		x	100
Lincoln	1947	5A-110		x	5
Magnavox	1924	TRF-5	x		225
	1925	TRF-5	x		250
Magnus	1925	"Magnutrol"	x		125
Majestic	1928	71 (console)		x	85
	1929	92		x	80
	1931	50		x	60
	1931	51		x	125
	1931	61		x	100
	1932	15A		x	65
	1932	200		x	90
	1933	194		x	125
	1933	331		x	85
	1933	336		x	115
	1933	370		x	75
	1933	371		x	80
	1933	463 "Century"		x	50
Mantola	1948	92516		x	5
Martinola	1924	Type I	x		100
Marwol	1925	"Jewel"	x		90
Metro	1925	"Metrodyne"	x		80
	1926	"Super 7"	x		200
Michigan	1923	"Junior"	x		125
Miraco	1923	K	x		65
Mitchell	1951	1254 "Madrigal"		x	6
Monitor	1947	TA56M		x	under 5
	1947	TC56M		x	7
	1947	TW56M		x	under 5
	1947	M-510 (portable)	x	x	under 5
	1948	RA50 (radio/phono)		x	20

Radio	Date	Model	Battery	A/C	Price
	1948	M3070 (AM/FM/phono)		x	$30
Motorola	1942	51X19		x	15
	1948	5A7 (portable)	x	x	under 5
	1948	47B11	x		under 5
	1948	56X11		x	under 5
	1948	57X11		x	under 5
	1948	58A11		x	8
	1948	67L11		x	under 5
	1948	67F11 (radio/phono)		x	12
	1948	67F12 (radio/phono)		x	10
	1948	75F31 (AM/FM/phono; console)		x	20
	1948	77XM22 (AM/FM)		x	15
	1949	58G11		x	5
	1949	67X		x	6
	1949	69L11		x	under 5
	1949	88FM21 (AM/FM/phono; console)		x	20
	1949	68F11 (radio/phono)		x	22
	1952	5H12		x	under 5
Mu-rad	1925	B	x		75
Murdock	1924	"Neutrodyne"	x		100
Ozarka	1924	RC200 (portable)	x		75
Packard Bell	1947	5DA		x	under 5
	1947	568 (radio/phono)		x	9
	1948	571;572		x	5
	1948	471 (portable)	x	x	under 5
Phanstiehl	1927	30	x		100
Philco	1928	511		x	95
	1928	525		x	100
	1928	551	x		125
	1929	87 (console)		x	200
	1930	20		x	100
	1930	20B		x	125
	1931	35	x		100
	1931	50		x	100
	1931	70B		x	125
	1931	70L (console)		x	70
	1931	90		x	125
	1931	90B		x	125
	1932	51B		x	125
	1933	14		x	40
	1933	38 (two band)	x		25
	1933	44 (four band)		x	140
	1933	54		x	45
	1933	57C		x	35
	1933	60B		x	70
	1933	66 (two band)		x	75
	1933	91		x	35
	1934	43		x	125
	1934	89B		x	105
	1934	200X (console		x	45
	1934	620 (multiband)	x		35
	1935	44		x	125
	1935	84		x	70

Radio	Date	Model	Battery	A/C	Price
	1936	116B (multiband)		x	$85
	1936	610 (AM/SW)		x	50
	1936	610T "Transitone" (two band)		x	40
	1936	620B (three band)		x	50
	1937*	37-38		x	80
	1937	37-61		x	55
	1937	37-84B "Baby Grand"		x	90
	1937	37-116 (console)		x	140
	1937	37-604 (two band)		x	20
	1937	37-620 (three band)		x	60
	1937	37-620CS (three band; chairside)		x	65
	1937	37-650		x	60
	1938	38-35		x	60
	1938	38-39 (two band)		x	75
	1938	38-116 (five band; console)		x	40
	1939	39-30T		x	30
	1939	39-61C		x	20
	1939	39-70	x		25
	1939	39-80	x		5
	1940	40-90	x		60
	1940	40-95	x		15
	1940	40-150 (three band)		x	35
	1942	42-650 (AM/SW/old FM)		x	20
	1942	42-1005 (two band/radio/phono; console)		x	60
	1942	42-PT88 (portable)	x	x	5
	1946	46-200		x	5
	1946	46-350 (portable)	x	x	15
	1946	46-427 (AM/SW)		x	12
	1946	46-1201 (radio/slip-in phono)		x	30
	1946	46-1203 (radio/phono)		x	30
	1947	47-1230 (AM/FM/SW/phono; console)		x	30
	1948	48-250		x	5
	1948	48-360 (portable)	x	x	6
	1948	48-461		x	5
	1948	48-472 (AM/FM)		x	7
	1948	48-482 (AM/FM/SW)		x	25
	1948	48-1270 (AM/FM/SW/phono; console)		x	25
	1948	48-1276 (AM/FM/phono)		x	50
	1948	48-1284 (two band/radio/phono)		x	25
	1949	49-101	x	x	11
	1949	49-500 "Transitone"		x	30
	1949	49-503		x	8
	1949	49-602 (portable)	x	x	5
	1949	49-900E		x	8
	1949	49-901		x	12
	1949	49-909		x	25
	1949	49-1401 (radio/slip-in phono)		x	25
	1950	50-524		x	9

*From 1937 on, dating Philco radios is easy because the number before the hyphen is the year the radio is made. The same model may have two different numbers, such as 39 and 40, if the same model was made in two different years.

Radio	Date	Model	Battery	A/C	Price
	1951	51-530		x	$ 5
RCA	1922	"Aeriola Jr." (crystal set)			125
	1922	"Aeriola Sr."	x		110
	1923	"Radiola Special"	x		150
	1923	"Radiola Sr."	x		175
	1924	"Radiola III"	x		100
	1924	"Radiola IIIA"	x		115
	1924	"Radiola X"	x		375
	1924	"Radiola AR-812"	x		85
	1924	"Radiola Super VIII"	x		225
	1925	"Radiola 20"	x		150
	1925	"Radiola 25"	x		250
	1925	"Radiola 26"	x		500
	1925	"Radiola 28"	x		125
	1927	"Radiola 18"		x	90
	1928	"Radiola 60"		x	85
	1929	"Radiola 33"		x	90
	1929	RE-45 (radio/phono) "Victor"		x	100
	1929	"Radiola 44"		x	65
	1933	143		x	100
	1933	28-D (tambour doors)		x	75
	1933	R28B "Carryette"		x	30
	1934	117 (two band)		x	70
	1934	121 (two band)		x	90
	1934	125 (two band)		x	40
	1934	128 (three band)		x	60
	1934	140		x	115
	1934	310 (radio/phono; console)		x	70
	1936	7T (three band)		x	50
	1936	85T		x	18
	1937	85E (chairside)		x	50
	1937	9K2 (five band; console)		x	40
	1938	97KG		x	60
	1938	811K (five band; console)		x	60
	1939	9TX-4		x	8
	1939	9TX-31 "Little Nipper"		x	12
	1939	94BP4 (portable)	x		under 5
	1939	94BT1	x		10
	1939	T-80 (three band)		x	65
	1940	45X1		x	8
	1941	28X (three band)		x	25
	1942	55X B-3251		x	15
	1946	68R1; 68R2		x	5
	1946	68R3		x	7
	1947	68R4		x	10
	1947	X60 (AM/SW)		x	11
	1947	Q36 (seven band)		x	30
	1947	Q103 (three band)		x	9
	1947	Q121 (five band)		x	15
	1947	61-6; 61-9		x	under 5
	1947	62-1 (radio/phono)		x	12
	1947	67V1 (AM/SW/phono; console)		x	30
	1947	85T8 (three band)		x	40

Radio	Date	Model	Battery	A/C	Price
	1947	515 (AM/SW)		x	$11
	1947	54B5 (portable)	x	x	under 5
	1948	65BR9 (portable)	x	x	under 5
	1948	65F	x		6
	1948	66X11; 66X12		x	5
	1948	66X13		x	8
	1948	66X14		x	under 5
	1948	66X15		x	9
	1948	Q122 (five band)		x	15
	1948	QB55X (three band)	x		5
	1948	QU72 (AM/SW/phono)		x	20
	1949	8R75 (AM/FM)		x	10
	1949	8V7 (radio/phono; console)		x	25
	1949	8X53		x	10
	1949	8X521		x	7
	1949	9X572		x	12
	1949	75X11		x	5
	1949	77U (radio/phono)		x	20
	1949	610V2 (AM/FM/phono)		x	25
	1949	Q109 (four band)		x	18
	1950	9X571		x	8
	1951	9Y511 (radio/45 rpm phono)		x	15
Radiodyne	1925	WC-11	x		200
Regal	1949	4963 (two band)		x	11
Remler	1937	46 "Scottie"		x	20
	1948	5300B "Scottie" (radio/phono)		x	8
	1949	5500 "Scottie Pup"		x	7
Robert-Lawrence	1948	102-L-6T		x	under 5
E.H. Scott					300-800+
Sentinel	1937	32B	x		25
	1937	76A (three band; console)		x	70
	1947	284GA (radio/phono)		x	15
	1947	286P (portable)	x	x	6
	1948	316PT (portable)	x	x	under 5
	1949	294-I		x	20
Setchell Carlson	1947	447 (portable)	x	x	under 5
	1948	408		x	6
	1948	437		x	6
	1949	469 (FM only)		x	18
Silvertone	1927	(no model number)	x		75
	1937	4420	x		15
	1937	4588 (four band; console)		x	35
	1938	6110		x	18
	1948	8005		x	6
	1950	9073 (radio/phono)		x	8
Sparton	1927	AC62		x	115
	1934	67 (two band)		x	40
	1934	75A (multiband)		x	40
	1938	1068 (three band; console)		x	40
Spitdorf	1925	R200	x		185
	1926	RV-580	x		140
Standardyne	1925	TRF	x		135
Steinite	1927	100	x		160

Radio	Date	Model	Battery	A/C	Price
	1930	410		x	$ 90
Stewart Warner	1925	300	x		100
	1929	900	x		95
	1935	1362 "Ferrodyne" (three band)		x	40
	1938	1822 (three band)		x	30
	1938	97-562		x	15
	1938	91-513		x	30
	1939	07-512 "Campus"		x	9
	1939	"Fireside"		x	25
Stromberg Carlson	1925	601	x		85
	1928	636A (console)		x	125
	1934	55 (console; remote control)		x	65
	1935	58T (three band)		x	60
	1937	127H (three band)		x	25
	1937	231-F (three band; coffee table)		x	55
	1937	231-R (three band; chairside)		x	60
	1939	410H (AM/SW)		x	30
Sylvania	1951	1-251		x	under 5
Tele-Tone	1948	150		x	6
	1948	152		x	5
	1948	156 (portable)	x		under 5
	1948	159		x	under 5
Terlee	1925	"Acme Reflex"	x		60
Thorola	1925	50 "Isodyne"	x		100
Trav-ler	1946	105		x	10
	1949	6053 (radio/phono)		x	8
Truetone	1948	D1850 (AM/FM/phono;console)		x	22
	1948	D2665	x		under 5
	1948	D2807		x	under 5
	1949	D1612		x	25
	1949	D2025A		x	12
	1949	D3809 (portable)	x		5
	1951	D1846 (AM/FM; console)		x	15
Tuska	1924	"Superdyne"	x		425
Westinghouse	1921	RA	x		150
	1929	WR-8-R (grandfather clock; remote control; not working)		x	250
	1934	WR-22			45
	1935	WR-602	x		40
	1935	WR-207 (two band)		x	30
	1935	WR-208 (two band)		x	30
	1946	H-171 (radio/phono; chairside)		x	30
	1947	H-148 (portable)	x	x	under 5
	1947	H-133	x		under 5
	1948	WR-478 (radio/phono)		x	15
	1948	H-202 (AM/FM)		x	13
	1948	H-188		x	12
	1948	H-165 (portable)	x	x	under 5
	1948	H-142 (five band)		x	22
	1948	H-157		x	9
	1948	H-178	x		5
	1949	H-161 (AM/FM)		x	15
	1949	H-182 (AM/FM)		x	10

Radio	Date	Model	Battery	A/C	Price
	1949	H-300T5		x	under 5
	1951	335T7U (AM/FM)		x	8
Woolaroc	1946	3-11A		x	20
Workrite	1927	37	x		100
Wurlitzer	1931	S-6 "Lyric"		x	150
	1934	SW88 "Lyric" (four band)		x	50
	1934	C-4LI "Lyric" (two band)		x	20
Zenith	1924	"Super Portable"	x		475
	1929	40A (radio/phono)		x	150
	1933	807 (two band)		x	50
	1933	711		x	85
	1933	712		x	75
	1934	"Stratosphere"		x	350+
	1934	740 (console)	x		20
	1934	6-V-27	x		30
	1935	835 (multiband)		x	235
	1935	5-S-119 (three band)		x	60
	1936	6-B-129	x		30
	1936	6-S-147 "Zephyr" (multiband; chairside)		x	65
	1937	5-R-317		x	65
	1937	6-S-222 (three band)		x	30
	1938	6-S-229		x	70
	1938	6-D-311		x	15
	1938	5-R-312		x	20
	1938	9-S-244 (three band; chairside)		x	70
	1939	4-K-331	x		16
	1946	8-H-061		x	65
	1946-1950	"Transoceanic" (several variations; portable)	x	x	45

The Adventures of Slim and Spud—"Music hath charms" but not at 2 a. m.

Glossary

A   heater or filament voltage for a tube. Supplied by battery or power supply.

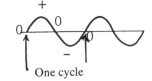
46. AC cycle.

AC (alternating current)   type of current in which the direction of the electron flow changes regularly at a rate measured in cycles per second, or hertz (figure 46).

Aerial   a conductor or system of conductors used for radiating or receiving radio waves.

Air cell   a type of battery cell used for an A voltage supply.

Alignment   the adjustment of receiver internal controls for the best reception of signals.

Ampere (amp.)   the unit of current flow. The current through a resistance of one ohm at an electrical pressure of one volt.

Amplification   the increase in the voltage, current, or power of a signal.

Antenna   aerial.

Arcing   electron current across a gap between two conductors.

Audio frequency (a.f.)   an audible frequency. About 20 to 20,000 cycles per second (hertz).

Audion   the vacuum tube developed by Dr. Lee DeForest.

Automatic volume control (AVC)   a method of maintaining the output volume of a receiver at a constant level, regardless of variations in the r.f. input signal strength.

B   the positive plate voltage used to draw electrons emitted by the cathode or filament to produce a useful current through a tube. It is supplied by battery or power supply.

Bakelite   trade name for a phenolic plastic used for insulation.

B eliminator   a B voltage power supply getting its energy from an AC power source.

Bias   a negative voltage applied between the grid and cathode of a tube to reduce current through the tube to a desired level.

Blocking condenser   a condenser used to keep direct current out of a circuit while passing alternating current.

Breakdown voltage   the voltage at which an insulator or dielectric will puncture, causing an electric arc and failure of the part.

Bypass condenser   a condenser used to provide an alternating current path around some circuit element.

C   negative voltage, called bias, applied between the grid of a tube and its cathode. Allows a tube to operate more accurately as an amplifier.

Cable   several insulated conductors within an outer covering.

Capacitor   a condenser. A device used to store small amounts of electrical energy. It will pass changes in charge level while resisting unchanging energy movement.

Carrier wave   the radio frequency output of a transmitter that may or may not be modulated by a signal.

Carrier frequency   the frequency of a transmitter's carrier wave.

Cathode   source of electron flow in a vacuum tube.

Center tap   the mechanical and electrical center of a transformer winding or a resistor.

Charge   the condition of having an excess or absence of electrons.

Chassis   the base (usually metal) on which a radio is built.

Choke coil   a coil having high inductance, which opposes alternating current while allowing passage of direct current.

Coil   a wire wound in a circular form that possesses inductance.

Component   a part of a circuit. (Examples: condenser, resistor, transformer, tube, speaker, tube socket, and so on.)

Condenser   a capacitor. Two conducting surfaces (plates) separated by an insulator (dielectric). If one plate receives a charge, the other plate will develop an opposite charge. Changing charges on one plate will cause a corresponding change on the other. Steady charges, such as a DC voltage, will charge the opposite place only once. No steady current will flow, but a varying current will.

Condenser capacity   the electrostatic storage ability of a condenser, measured in farads.

Condenser leakage   a small flow of current through a condenser with a faulty dielectric.

Conductor a material that allows current to flow through it easily when a voltage is applied between its ends.

Contact points the metal parts of a switch that complete a circuit when they touch.

Crystal detector a detector that operates through the rectifying qualities of certain minerals.

Current electron flow.

Cycle one complete positive and one complete negative alternation of an alternating current. Measured in cycles per second or hertz.

DC (direct current) an electrical current in which the flow of electrons is always in one direction.

Demodulation the process of detection of a modulated wave, current, or voltage, in order to obtain the signal given it in the modulation process.

Detector (demodulator) device removing radio frequency part of a signal, leaving its audio portion.

Dielectric a nonconducting medium. Any insulation between two conductors permitting electrostatic attraction and repulsion to take place across it.

Diode a two-element device, usually a vacuum tube or crystal, that rectifies a current. It acts as a valve allowing current to flow in one direction only.

Distortion an unfaithful reproduction of the original wave form of a signal.

Dry cell a chemical cell producing 1.5 volts.

Dynamic loudspeaker a moving coil loudspeaker.

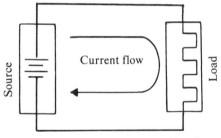

47. Electrical circuit (source and load).

Electric circuit a complete conductive path permitting electron flow (figure 47).

Electrolytic condenser a condenser in which the electrolyte and an electrode serve as plates. The dielectric is a film formed by electrolysis. Condenser has a high capacity and is used for power supply filter and audio frequency bypass.

Electron the negative portion of an atom. The moving portion of an electric current.

Element one of the electrodes (working parts) of a tube or other device.

Emission electron release from a heated cathode or filament.

Farad (f.) the unit of measurement of capacity.

Feedback the transfer of energy from the output to the input of the same circuit.

Field coil the magnetic coil producing the magnetic force in a type of dynamic speaker.

Filament a directly heated electron emitter in a vacuum tube.

Filament circuit all parts through which filament heating current flows.

Filament rheostat a variable resistance used to regulate the voltage to the filament of a tube. In some old sets it is used for volume control.

Filter choke an inductance used in a power supply to filter out DC variations (ripple).

Filter condenser the condenser used in a filter system to pass alternating or ripple currents to ground while keeping the direct current (B+) in the circuit.

First detector in a superheterodyne receiver, the tube in which the received signal is mixed with a signal generated in the set to form an intermediate frequency.

Frequency the number of cycles per second of an alternating current.

Front panel the surface on which most working controls for a receiver are placed.

Full wave rectifier a two-section rectifier, arranged so current is allowed to pass to the load in the same direction during each half cycle of the AC supply. One part works during one-half cycle, and the other during the next.

Fuse a protective device that will break the circuit if excessive current flows within it.

Gain the ratio of the output to the input of an amplifier, of power, current, or voltage.

Gang condenser two or more variable condensers operating from one control shaft.

Grid a wire coil or screen between the cathode and plate of a tube. When charged it acts to retard or aid the flow of electrons from that cathode to the plate.

Grid circuit the grid and cathode of a tube, together with all parts connecting them.

Grid current detection the signal is rectified in the grid circuit. Grid current flows through a high resistance, varying the bias on the tube at the modulation frequency. The tube amplifies the bias change.

Grid lead a resistance in the grid circuit of a tube that permits excess electrons to leak off the grid after each charge. Electrons accumulating on the grid would eventually block the tube, preventing operation.

Grid lead detector a tube accomplishing grid current detection.

Ground the earth and all parts of a circuit connected directly to it.

Heater the electric heater that heats the cathode of a tube, allowing the cathode to emit electrons.

Henry the unit of electrical inductance.

Hertz (H) a unit of frequency equal to one cycle per second.

Heterodyne the combination of two separate frequencies.

Impedance the total opposition of a circuit to alternating current, due to resistance and reactance. Measured in ohms.

Inductance character of a circuit opposing any change in current flow. Measured in henrys.

Inductive reactance the opposition of a pure inductance to the flow of alternating current. Measured in ohms.

Inductor a coil.

Input the point at which power is put into a device, or the power that is introduced.

Insulation material used to prevent the flow of current between conductors.

Interference any undesired noise or signal entering a receiver.

i.f. (intermediate frequency) the frequency produced by combining a locally generated signal and the carrier signal it is desired to receive. In superheterodyne receivers, this provides a new signal frequency that can be better amplified and tuned, improving reception.

Intermittent an irregular or occasional contact or connection within a circuit caused by shorting, loose connections, or other faults.

Interstage transformer a transformer used to couple two vacuum tube stages together.

Kilocycle 1000 cycles per second.

Kilohertz (kH.) kilocycle.

Lead a conductor attached to an electrical device.

Lead in connection between antenna and receiver.

Line a conductor supplying current to a load some distance from its source.

Load place where electron flow does work (see figure 47).

Local oscillations any oscillating currents generated in a receiver.

48. Loop antenna.

Loop antenna an antenna of continuous turns of wire on a supporting frame (figure 48).

Loudspeaker a device for converting audio frequency current into sound waves.

Megahertz (mH.) a unit of frequency equal to 1,000,000 hertz.

Mica condenser a high quality condenser with mica dielectric.

Microfarad (mfd.) a useful unit of capacity in radio work, which is 1/1,000,000 of a farad. A micromicrofarad (mmfd.) is 1/1,000,000 of a microfarad.

Microphonic condition existing when mechanical vibrations affect a tube causing sounds in its output.

Milli- prefix meaning one one-thousandth. (1 milliamp = 1/1,000 or .001 ampere.)

Mixer tube a tube in which a locally generated frequency is combined with the carrier signal frequency to obtain a desired intermediate frequency.

Modulated wave a continuous wave, the amplitude or frequency of which is varied in accordance with the signal to be transmitted.

Motorboating a low frequency audio oscillation in an amplifier usually caused by coupling between stages through the power supply, which makes a putt-putt sound.

Negative any potential lower than another that is taken as a reference. Example: -6 volts is negative to -2 volts.

Neutralizing the application of out of phase feedback to an amplifier to prevent oscillation.

Neutrodyne receiver a receiver using neutralized tuned radio frequency amplifier stages.

ohm the unit of electrical resistance. The value of resistance permitting the flow of one ampere of current to one volt of pressure.

Ohmmeter an instrument for measuring resistance, calibrated in ohms.

Ohm's law defines the relationship of voltage (E), current (I), and resistance (R) in a circuit. Expressed as I=E/R.

Open no electrical connection where one could or should exist.

Oscillating alternately surging first in one direction and then in the reverse. Caused in a vacuum tube by feeding a portion of the output into its input.

Oscillating circuit a circuit that contains inductance and capacity in which a voltage impulse produces a regularly reversing current.

Oscillator a device for producing oscillating currents of a frequency determined by the physical constants of the circuit.

Output power from a circuit sent to a load.

Output transformer the iron core transformer coupling the power tube to a loudspeaker.

p.m. speaker a dynamic speaker with a magnetic field produced by a strong permanent magnet. Used in most modern sets.

Paper condenser a condenser using a paper dielectric.

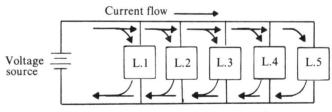

49. Parallel circuit.

Parallel circuit a group of components through which power flows through individual, separate loads (figure 49).

Pentode a five-element vacuum tube.

Permanent magnet a hardened piece of magnetized steel that will hold its magnetism indefinitely.

Plate collector for electrons in a vacuum tube. Given positive charge.

Plate bypass condenser a condenser in parallel with the load of a detector tube to bypass r.f. currents to ground, leaving audio frequencies unchanged.

Plate circuit the entire path through which a tube's plate current flows.

Plate condenser a DC blocking condenser in the plate circuit of a tube.

Plate current the direct current flowing between the cathode and the plate of a tube.

Plate current detection detection obtained by operating the detector with a high grid bias. As a result, the average plate current varies at the audio modulation frequency.

Plate voltage the positive DC potential between the plate and cathode of a tube, called the B voltage.

Polarity characteristic of a device that has or requires a certain positive or negative charge at certain points. Example: Both batteries and electrolytic condensers have plus or minus poles.

Positive a shortage of electrons with respect to earth or another part of a circuit.

Potential the presence of electrons in excess or in fewer numbers than another point in a circuit produces an electrical pressure, called potential or voltage difference.

Potentiometer a variable resistance voltage divider. Often used as a volume control.

Power amplifier an amplifier designed to furnish power to a loudspeaker.

Power supply a source for necessary operating voltages for a receiver. Sometimes called a battery eliminator, it receives its operating power from the AC power line.

Primary winding the winding of a transformer to which power is applied.

Push pull amplification two tubes used in such a way that each provides output during the half cycle when the other is not amplifying or is operating out of phase.

Radiation the transmission of energy in wave form through a medium. In the case of radio, space.

r.f. (radio frequency) any frequency higher than about 50,000 cycles per second.

r.f. choke an inductance coil offering a high opposition to radio frequency currents.

r.f. oscillator a device that produces sustained oscillations at radio frequencies. It is usually in the form of a tuned circuit activated by a vacuum tube.

r.f. transformer a transformer designed to operate at radio frequencies.

Radio spectrum all frequencies capable of radiation.

Radio wave an electromagnetic wave that travels through space.

Reactance the opposition to the flow of alternating current by the inductance of a coil, the capacity of a condenser, or a combination of both.

Rectification the process of producing direct current from alternating current.

Rectifier a device that changes alternating current into pulsating direct current (figure 50).

Reflex circuit a circuit arrangement in which the signal is amplified, both before and after detection, in the same amplifier tubes.

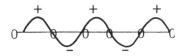

Alternating current

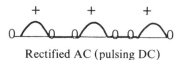

Rectified AC (pulsing DC)

50. Alternating current and rectified AC (pulsing DC).

Regeneration increasing the energy input to a tube by feeding back part of the output into the input to be reamplified.

Regenerative detector a vacuum tube detector in which regeneration is used to increase sensitivity by plate to grid coupling.

Resistance the opposition to a flow of current. Measured in ohms.

Resistor a unit offering a definite electrical resistance.

Resonance the condition existing when the capacitive reactance and the inductive reactance are in exact opposition.

Resonant frequency the frequency at which the inductive and capacitive reactance in a circuit become equal and cancel each other.

Rheostat a variable resistance.

Screen grid a grid placed between the control grid and the plate of a tube. Reduces tendency of tube to oscillate.

Second detector the tube that detects the intermediate frequency in a superheterodyne receiver.

Secondary circuit a circuit obtaining its energy by induction from another circuit.

Selectivity the ability of a receiver to tune to a particular frequency while rejecting others.

Sensitivity the degree to which a receiver responds to a given signal.

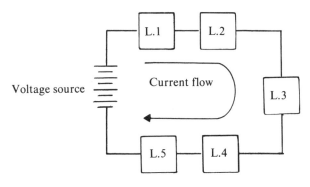

51. Series circuit.

Series circuit several loads arranged so that power flows through each in turn (figure 51).

Sharp tuning having a high degree of selectivity.

Shield a conducting metal enclosure, attached to circuit ground, used to protect a circuit from the effects of external magnetic or electrical fields.

Short circuit (short) direct electrical connection where none should exist.

Short wave generally, frequencies higher than 3,000 kilocycles.

Source location where an electrical current or signal originates (figure 47).

Stage a tube and its associated parts affecting a signal passing through it.

Superheterodyne receiver a receiver in which the transmitted signal is mixed with a signal generated in the receiver, producing an intermediate frequency that is always the same. This intermediate frequency is amplified, tuned, and detected to reproduce the original audio frequency.

Switch a device for changing the connections of a circuit.

Tetrode a four-element tube.

Tickler coil a winding used to couple the plate circuit of a tube with its grid circuit in a regenerative detector.

Tone control any method of emphasizing either high or low tones at will.

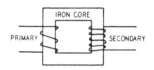

52. Basic transformer.

Transformer two or more windings with a common magnetic circuit, allowing the transfer of power by magnetic induction. Used to transfer power, increasing or decreasing its voltage, between two circuits (figure 52).

Trimmer condenser a small, adjustable condenser in parallel with a tuning condenser or coil for aligning a tuned circuit with other circuits in a receiver.

Triode a tube with three working elements.

Tuned circuit a circuit with parts selected to resonate at a certain frequency. That frequency may be a) reinforced, b) selected (and others rejected), or c) reduced in strength (trapped), depending on how the circuit is used.

Tuned radio frequency amplification (TRF) amplification of radio frequency signal with coupling between stages provided by air core transformers with secondary windings tuned to resonate with the incoming radio frequency by tuning condensers.

Tuning adjusting a circuit by varying its inductance or capacity to select a certain desired frequency while rejecting all other frequencies. The circuit is made to resonate at the desired frequency.

Tuning coil an inductance coil in a circuit that may be tuned to resonance by varying its inductance.

Tuning condenser a variable capacity condenser having one or more sets of fixed plates and one or more sets of rotating plates. It is adjusted to resonate with a fixed inductance at the desired frequency.

Vacuum tube a device consisting of a number of electrodes contained within a high vacuum enclosure.

Variable condenser any condenser whose capacity can be changed during operation.

Vario-coupler an inductive coupling with the secondary coil arranged to rotate inside the primary coil and thus vary the amount of magnetic coupling between the two.

Vernier dial a device by which a complete turn of the control knob turns a shaft only part of a turn.

Voice coil a light coil attached to the cone of a dynamic speaker. The signal voltage in the coil reacts to the strong magnetic field surrounding it, moving the cone in proportion to the audio frequency voltage applied to it.

Volt (v.) the practical unit of electrical force. The electrical pressure that will cause one ampere of current to flow through a resistance of one ohm.

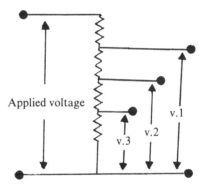

53. Voltage divider.

Voltage divider a series of resistances between a positive and negative source that divides out certain lower voltages (v.1, v.2, v.3 in figure 53) for a receiver.

Voltage drop the difference between voltages at two points in a circuit.

Voltage rating the maximum regular voltage at which a device may be operated without damage.

Voltmeter an instrument that measures the voltage between two points.

Volume the degree of loudness of sound produced by a loudspeaker.

Volume control a device for regulating the intensity of volume.

Watt the unit of electrical power equal to a current of one amp at a pressure of one volt.

Wavelength the distance between two successive peaks of the same polarity on a wave. Usually measured in meters.

Winding the wire forming a coil.

Wire-wound resistor resistance wire-wound on an insulating form.

Index

About the Authors

David is an ex-radio engineer, now a minister, who still likes working with radios. Betty is a librarian who enjoys refinishing furniture. Putting their interests together, they got into the business of repairing and restoring old radios. They are concerned about the fine old radios moldering in attics and garages that could be saved and enjoyed today.

David is the author of *Guidelines: Thoughts on Christian Country Living*, a collection of his *Wallaces Farmer* religious articles published in book form by the Wallace-Homestead Book Company.